Come, Let Us Pray!

J. Emmette Weir

Come, Let Us Pray!

J. Emmette Weir

Unless otherwise noted, all Scripture quotations are from the King James Version of the Bible. Quotations marked NEB are from the New English Bible. Quotations marked GN are from Good News for Modern Man, Today's English Version. Quotations marked RSV are from the Revised Standard Version of the Bible.

Copyright © 1993 by J. Emmette Weir

Printed in the United States of America
ISBN 1-56229-202-1

Pneuma Life Publishing
P.O. Box 10612
Bakersfield, CA 93389
(805) 324-1741

Contents

Dedication
Acknowledgments
Foreword
Introduction

Endnotes
Appendix

Dedication

In Loving Memory of:
Eunice Jeanette Weir
1910-1965
great teacher
great mother
great Christian
and
Sister Zoe Knowles
a great woman of prayer
and to
my dear, loving father
Gaspar Emmett Weir
and to
the many prayer warriors
who participated in
The Bahamas National Call To Prayer
1991-1992

Acknowledgments

The apostle Paul, writing to a small Christian community, asked this challenging, thought-provoking question: "What do you possess that was not given to you?" (1 Cor. 4:7, NEB). This letter, written nearly two thousand years ago, reminds us of this profound truth: No matter what we achieve in our journey through life, we are greatly indebted to others!

This is certainly true of this work, which would not have been possible without the encouragement, support, and labors of many persons whom the Lord has used, sometimes in unexpected ways, to help me in the production of this book.

I would like to express my deep gratitude to "the faithful few" members of Ebenezer Methodist Church, East Shirley Street, Nassau, Bahamas, who attended the prayer meetings on Tuesday evenings and Thursday mornings, whose spiritual endeavors first inspired me to begin work on a book on prayer while ministering there (1981-1986). Mr. Alfred Stewart, a dynamic Christian layman, prominent Bahamian banker, and organizer of the Bahamas National Call to Prayer 1991-1992, greatly encouraged me in preparing the material for this book.

Mrs. Ava Forber and Mrs. Lynn Armstrong, secretaries at Templeton Theological Seminary, transformed my poorly executed typescript into a neat, legible product with unfailing patience and consummate skill. Mrs. Earthel L. Smith, working with deft skill and a smile, committed it to a word processor. Mr. Wellington Chea edited the manuscript. Sir Leonard Knowles, Mr. Oswald

Munnings, and Mrs. Lily Weir-Coakley, librarian, assisted in proof-reading.

Mr. Bertram Knowles, Captain Durward "Sea Wolf" Knowles, and Mrs. Dianne M. Kemp gave me encouragement and practical assistance. I also thank The Rev. Wilbert Forker, Chairman, Board of Trustees, Templeton Theological Seminary, a school of theology in the commonwealth of the Bahamas; and Sir John Templeton, moving spirit behind the prestigious Templeton Prize for Progress in Religion and Templeton Theological Seminary.

This work has also been influenced by Dr. Myles Munroe, President of Bahamas Faith Ministries, and Dr Kevin Alcena, President, Alcena Credit International Corporation and The McHari Institute, an international educational foundation based in Nassau, Bahamas. My thanks also go to Evangelist Rex Major, the Rev. Dr. Fr. Patrick Pinder, The Rev. Dr. Charles Smith, and the Ven. Archdeacon William Thompson, all clergymen serving in the Bahamas, and Mrs. Genevieve Luna, assistant librarian, The Stitt Library, Austin Presbyterian Theological Seminary, Austin, Texas, for their kind assistance in compiling the list of additional resources for the development of one's prayer life.

Finally, to Ena, my dear faithful wife; Ellsworth and Erica, who, though not complaining, just wondered why "Daddy was typing so much!" To God be the glory, great things He hath done!

Foreword

Prayer moves the hand that moves the world. Our greatest strength in this world can be found in praying to a God who has all power, all wisdom, and all knowledge. In fact, He is the very essence and source of all that exists.

Being the God of the spirits of all flesh (Numbers 16:22), God deeply cares for and desires to communicate with His children. He invites us to "come boldly unto the throne of grace, that we may obtain mercy, and find grace to help in time of need" (Hebrews 4:16).

God asks His people, "Am I a God at hand, . . . and not a God afar off?" (Jer. 23:23). He has provided many precious promises for His children:

Ask, and it shall be given you; seek, and ye shall find; knock, and it shall be opened unto you: For every one that asketh receiveth; and he that seeketh findeth; and to him that knocketh it shall be opened (Matthew 7:7,8).

And this is the confidence that we have in him, that, if we ask anything according to his will, he heareth us: And if we know that he hear us, whatsoever we ask, we know that we have the petitions that we desired of him (1 John 5:14,15).

God is love and love is God. His love is evident by His willingness to comfort or assist us in our journey through this world.

Prayer is more than receiving, however. Prayer is also an opportunity to live in divine, intimate communion with a God whose eyes simultaneously observe the ways of all mankind and yet know your most intimate needs.

Dr. Weir's book, *Come, Let Us Pray!*, is a classic. His scholastic training and personal experiences deliver treasures of wisdom and applicable knowledge on the subject of prayer. Going beyond the mechanics of prayer, he explains the true meaning, vitality, and power that prayer can bring to anyone who desires a more fulfilling life.

Derwin Stewart
President, Pneuma Life Publishing

Introduction

"Lord, teach us to pray, as John also taught his disciples" (Luke 11:1). The disciples of Jesus came to Him with this simple request. These disciples, who had spent much time with the Master and most certainly had witnessed Him often at prayer, wanted Him to teach them to pray.

It is noteworthy that they did not ask Him to teach them to preach, or to do pastoral visitation, or even to heal, though it is recorded that there were times when they experienced difficulty in exercising the healing ministry (Mark 9:14-19; Matthew 17:14-21; Luke 9:37-45). They specifically asked Him to teach them to pray!

That shows us something very significant. If they requested lessons in prayer, they thought that such instruction was essential. Why did the disciples ask the Master to teach them to pray?

When we reflect upon the nature and meaning of prayer, it is not at all difficult to understand the reason for this request. Prayer is at once very simple and most profound.

One of the great hymn writers of the Church said, "Prayer is the soul's sincere desire uttered or unexpressed." This definition gives us much to think about, for prayer is essentially a deeply spiritual matter. Prayer is at the heart of mankind's spiritual quest.

Prayer is, in one sense, very simple. Even a small child can pray to God. Indeed, sometimes we are amazed at the spiritual insight that children display in their prayer, especially at bedtime.

On the other hand, prayer is a tremendous spiritual exercise that requires years of practice. Even the most spiritual, seasoned Christians confess that they still have much to learn about prayer. Indeed, it is impossible to describe or understand prayer adequately. All we know is that in prayer we are drawn very near to God, and almost instinctively, we bring our concerns to Him.

Since prayer is so simple that even a little child can do it but so profound that even the most experienced Christians cannot plumb its spiritual depths, we must do everything that we possibly can to improve the quality of our prayer life. In other words, *prayer can be learned.* By practice we can improve our prayer life and, therefore, our spiritual walk with God.

Our purpose in this book is to explore the various aspects of prayer with a view to improving the quality of our prayer life. First, we will look at the main elements of prayer: praise, thanksgiving, petition, confession, and intercession. We will also discuss how to respond when encountering problems in our prayer life. We will explore the nature of prayer in terms of listening. Finally, we will offer some practical hints that may help us to improve our prayer life.

Properly used, this book should contribute greatly to enriching the spiritual development of the reader.

Chapter 1

What is Prayer?

If you were to ask a group of people, "What is prayer?" you would probably get as many answers as persons in the group. Prayer can be defined in many different ways. For instance, the participants in a session on prayer offered some of the following definitions:

Prayer is a family conversing with God.

Prayer is saying "I'm sorry" to God and asking for grace not to repeat our failure.

Prayer is a child's simplest form of communication with God.

Prayer is talking to God.

Prayer is bringing to God my deep concern for those who are near me – my family and friends.

Prayer is the way to inner peace.

"And the prayer of faith shall save the sick."

Prayer is laying before God a concern for our enemies.

Prayer is work.

Prayer is where our hopes are confirmed and faith is enriched.

Prayer is a deep, unuttered desire within a human heart.[1]

As we examine these varied definitions of prayer, reflect upon others you have heard elsewhere. Think about your own definition of prayer. Can we discern a common idea linking them, in some way, with one another? Is there a recurring theme that emerges as the meaning of prayer is examined in depth? The answer – communion with God!

Yes, it may be confidently asserted that prayer is, first and foremost, communion with God. "Metropolitan Anthony," alias Anthony Bloom, a bishop of the Russian Orthodox Church in Great Britain, offers these spiritual insights:

> *Prayer is primarily an encounter with God. On certain occasions we may be aware of God's presence, more often dimly so, but there are times when we can place ourselves before Him only by an act of faith, without being aware of His presence at all. It is not the degree of our awareness that is relevant, that makes this encounter possible and fruitful; other conditions must be fulfilled, the basic one being that the person should be real.*[2]

In prayer, then, we draw near to God; we seek to enter into an intimate relationship with our Maker. In prayer, we humbly approach God, expressing our inmost thoughts and cherished secrets – things we dare to reveal only to our closest friends. The psalmist expressed it very well in these words:

> *Trust in him at all times; ye people, pour out your heart before him: God is a refuge for us (Psalm 62:8).*

God also draws near to us in prayer, making it the supreme form of communion between God and man. God comes to meet us where we are. He graciously condescends to dwell with us as we aspire to meet Him.

Prayer is utterly essential for spiritual growth. John Wesley, a giant of the devotional life who arose at 4:00 a.m. each day to pray, often urged his fellow Christians, "Do not neglect the means of grace!" Among these means of grace, prayer occupies a place of prime importance. It is written, "We perish if we cease from prayer." This is indeed the case. Spiritually, we do perish when we neglect prayer, for we lack nourishment for our souls. This is why the apostle Paul exhorts us to "pray without ceasing" (1 Thess. 5:17).

Prayer, then, is an intensely spiritual experience! Prayer is natural; it is "second nature" to man because man is a spiritual being. The Bible tells us that "the Lord God . . . breathed into his nostrils the breath of life; and man became a living soul" (Genesis 2:7). This living soul, the spiritual aspect of man, is nourished in communion with God. Prayer is the chief means of this spiritual nourishment. In a sense, prayer is to the soul what breathing is to the body – the means by which it is sustained. Yes, prayer is essential for the nurture of the soul.

If you were to ask a deeply spiritual person why he or she devotes so much time to prayer, the answer would simply be, "I can't help it!" Prayer is so natural for the true Christian that he does not have to learn it. Yet, in a deeper sense, he still has to keep learning more about prayer so that it may continue to be a source of spiritual growth and strength. In earnest prayer we are strengthened as we wait upon the Lord.

The prophet Isaiah declared:

But they that wait upon the Lord shall renew their strength; they shall mount up with wings as eagles; they shall run, and not be weary; they shall walk, and not faint (Isaiah 40:31).

Prayer, the greatest source of spiritual power, draws us into a deep, abiding, and refreshing communion with our God. Mere words cannot adequately express the depth of our spiritual joy or the height of our ecstasy as we dwell continually in the divine presence in prayer. How profound our joy, how elevated our spirits when we commune with the Lord as "friend to friend."

As the hymn writer said, we really do bear much needless pain and sorrow when we do not allow the Spirit of God to envelop us in prayer! We have the duty and the great privilege to constantly seek the divine presence in prayer. There is no sweeter communion than that which we experience in deep and earnest prayer.

Because prayer is so intensely personal, no two persons can have precisely the same experience. Each person has to come to his or her understanding in the context of a personal encounter with the

Living God. This is precisely why we cannot really describe the experience of prayer to anyone else. In the final analysis, the best we can do is to testify of the great benefits that we have received as a result of our communion with God.

Yes, we can join with the psalmist in inviting them: "O taste and see that the Lord is good" (Psalm 34:8).

Therefore, we must take time to pray. It is essential that we find time to retire from our daily duties and the pressures of "making a living" to be with the Lord. How easy it is for us to become so obsessed with "making a living" that we devote so very little time to "making life worth living!"

God desires to draw us into a deep, satisfying relationship with Himself. In such moments, alone with our Maker, we are refreshed and strengthened to carry out our daily tasks with enthusiasm and sincerity, and in a manner that brings glory to Christ. As we leave the place of earnest prayer – the place of "wrestling with God" – like Jacob, we are strengthened to continue our daily endeavors with the best of our ability, with concern for others, and to the glory of God!

Let us seek to be continually in communion with the Master by means of prayer! As we continually abide in the inner chamber, that place "near to the heart of God," we will truly find rest, recreation, and restoration for our weary souls. Let us not be satisfied with second best. Let us dwell continually in the divine presence where we shall experience tremendous spiritual growth.

O the pure delight of a single hour
That before Thy throne I spend,
When I kneel in prayer, and with Thee, my God,
I commune as friend with friend.
Draw me nearer, nearer, blessed Lord,
To the Cross where Thou hast died:
Draw me nearer, nearer, nearer, blessed Lord,
To thy precious, bleeding side.[3]
Frances Jean van Alystyne, 1820-1915

Summary

What can we say about prayer?

1. Prayer is essentially communion with God.

2. Prayer is very simple.

3. Prayer is very profound.

4. Prayer is a means of grace by which we aspire to reach God. He chooses to meet us at our point of need.

5. Prayer is essential for spiritual growth.

Chapter 2

Prayer is Praise

The rays of the tropical sun shone brilliantly through the window panes of the main church in a small village located on the north coast of the Caribbean isle. A hush of expectation descended upon the large, predominantly youthful congregation as it waited for the Sunday worship service to begin.

Why such enthusiasm this morning? Today was Youth Sunday, and the young people of the church would conduct each facet of the service.

The choir, consisting mainly of young people in their teens, was dressed in their brightly colored summer uniforms. Then a young preacher ascended the pulpit and announced the call to worship:

"Enter into his gates with thanksgiving, and into his courts with praise: be thankful unto him, and bless his name" (Psalm 100:4).

The youth choir arose and burst forth into the well-known sacred song of praise: "Praise Him! Praise Him! Praise Him! Praise Him!"

The choristers were enjoying worship! Rocking to the rhythm of the music, they indeed made "a joyful noise unto the Lord," as the young organist demonstrated his mastery of the keyboard and the other musicians formed a small band playing the drums, guitar, and tambourine. They continued singing, "Praise Him! Praise Him! For He is worthy to be praised!"[1]

The whole congregation, deeply inspired by the singing of the choir, soon joined with its members in praising the Lord. As the song ended, they responded with shouts of "Amen!" and "Praise the Lord!"

Considering the atmosphere that prevailed, it's not surprising that the congregation joined the choir in singing praise to the Lord. Praising Almighty God is at the very heart of worship. Indeed, it is the essence of worship.

What is Praise?

Praise, from a deeply spiritual perspective, may best be described as the human response to the realization of the greatness of God. When we reflected upon the meaning of prayer in the opening chapter, we saw that it is essentially communion with God. As we think more deeply about the meaning of communion with God, we come to understand the nature of praise.

The greatness of God as Creator of all things is profoundly expressed in the opening words of Scripture:

In the beginning God created the heaven and the earth. And the earth was without form, and void; and darkness was upon the face of the deep. And the Spirit of God moved upon the face of the waters (Genesis 1:1,2).

As we continue to read and meditate upon this opening chapter of Scripture, we are moved to acknowledge His greatness and to proclaim His sustaining grace. Indeed, this theme is repeated throughout the Bible. The reader is exhorted to praise God for His wondrous, creative activity and His sustaining power.

That well-known song of praise, "How Great Thou Art," also illustrates that contemplating on the greatness of God leads us to offer praise to our Creator. Indeed, who can meditate on the greatness of God as expounded in Scripture and the hymns of the Church without bursting into praise?

Moreover, when we reflect upon the purpose of our existence, we are led to appreciate the meaning of praise. The Book of Genesis teaches us that mankind has been created in the divine image. Referring to the pinnacle of the creative process, the Bible declares, "So God created man in his own image, in the image of God created he him; male and female created he them" (Genesis 1:27).

This gives us the basis of the Judeo-Christian conviction that a deep, intimate relationship exists between God and man – the supreme relationship.

Having been created in the image of God, mankind realizes its true potential in communion with God. Concisely, man is incomplete without God. Or, as Augustine put it: "O Lord, Thou has created us for Thyself, and our hearts are restless until they find their rest in Thee."[2]

Many ask the question, "What is the purpose of human existence?" The answer, from the Christian perspective, comes to us in the words of the Westminster Confession: "The true end of man is to worship the Lord and to enjoy Him forever."

This is just another way of saying that the meaning of human existence is to be found in communion with God. Praise, fundamentally speaking, is the highest activity in which mankind can engage. In praising God, we join the patriarchs, priests, and prophets. The saints who have passed on before us worship with the saints who are alive. Yes, all of creation acknowledges the majesty, holiness, and graciousness of God our Creator.

We praise the God of Love who revealed Himself in Jesus Christ. In His presence we become aware of the operation of the Holy Spirit in our lives. Indeed, there is no more noble, no more satisfying, no more nourishing and edifying source of spiritual strength than the pure, unadulterated praise of God!

Praise takes a number of forms, including:

Singing

Singing is one of the main ways of praising God. No one who has sung with a large congregation of enthusiastic worshipers can doubt this! Singing is related to the Christian doctrine of creation, since we acknowledge that the use of our voices is one of God's greatest gifts to mankind. Acknowledging God as our Creator, we render praise with our voices. The youth choir in that village church in the Caribbean also used the gift of music as a means of praising God.

Many of the psalms were songs of praise used in worship at the temple in Israel. Indeed, a number of our hymns of praise are really psalms that have been adapted for worship in a modern setting. Consider, for instance, the Scottish paraphrase of Psalm 100:

> *All people that on earth do dwell,*
> *Sing to the Lord with cheerful voice:*
> *Him serve with mirth, His praise forth tell:*
> *Come ye before Him and rejoice.*

Clapping

The clapping of the hands is another way of praising God in worship. Very often, clapping accompanies singing. Clapping, which has often been associated with the more charismatic forms of worship, is becoming accepted in the more liturgical traditions. Significantly, clapping played an important part in worship in ancient Israel. One of the major enthronement psalms begins: "Clap your hands, all you nations; acclaim our God with shouts of joy" (Psalm 47:1, NEB).

Lifting the Hands

The lifting of hands in praise is very closely related to, and often accompanies, clapping. While it has been perceived as a method used in charismatic worship, it is gaining wide acceptance among all Christian denominations. Significantly, lifting the hands also has biblical sanction:

Behold, bless ye the Lord, all ye servants of the Lord, which by night stand in the house of the Lord. Lift up your hands in the sanctuary, and bless the Lord! (Psalm 134:1,2).

Playing Musical Instruments

Musical instruments greatly enhance our ability to praise God. In modern Western Christianity, the organ has been the main instrument used in worship. Today, however, many more instruments are being accepted as authentic means of rendering praise to God. These include the guitar, trumpet, drums, and other percussion instruments such as the tambourine, in addition to the instrument that is traditionally used in worship – the organ. Scripture gives us a strong warrant for the use of many musical instruments, which can be verified by even a cursory reading of Psalms. Psalm 150, for instance, mentions at least half a dozen musical instruments.

Dancing

Dancing, another method of worship, is becoming more recognized in contemporary worship. The Bible sanctions this expression of praise. David "danced before the Lord" (2 Samuel 6:14). Significantly, in churches of many varied denominations, dancing is being utilized in worship. In their efforts to appeal to youth, churches all over the world are seeking to make worship an interesting and exciting experience.

Worship as Affirmation

We must remember that worship is essentially a dialogue between the worshiping community and the Lord. The leader(s) and congregation join in offering praise to God. If worship is to be truly effective, the one who leads in worship must enjoy rapport and communication with the members of his or her congregation. Indeed, it is a corporate experience in which they draw inspiration from God and are uplifted as they worship together. Anyone who has participated in an inspiring service can testify to the validity of this fact.

This is precisely why most orders of service provide for some form of response by the congregation. The leader and congregation may read verses of Scripture alternately. Some liturgical traditions include written responses for the congregation, which correspond to a bidding by the leader(s).

In some services, depending on their approach to worship, there is a strong element of spontaneous response. During the prayers, after the singing of a hymn or selection by the choir or soloist, or even during the sermon, members of the congregation may respond audibly with shouts of "Amen" (which is Hebrew for "So be it!") or with "Hallelujah" (which means "Praise the Lord!" in Hebrew). Sometimes the response is not audible; the listeners may simply be nodding the head in approval. When a member of the congregation responds in this way, he or she participates in the worship of God and even assists the leader. In virtually all forms of worship today, affirmation is being more widely accepted.

Prayer

People seek many ways to engage in their most exalted task – the praise of Almighty God. As has been demonstrated throughout the ages, however, prayer is the most effective, the most frequently used, the most profound, and the most deeply satisfying way of giving expression to the human yearning to praise God. Praise is at the heart of worship. Moreover, as we participate in prayer day by day and draw near to God, we realize that praise is an essential element of prayer.

As we begin prayer, we are naturally led to offer praise to the God of our salvation. Why is it so important to include the element of praise in our prayer?

First, praise forms a most fitting introduction to prayer. Our prayer, if it is to be meaningful and spiritually uplifting, should begin with a word of praise, of acknowledging God's divine creativity and that He is the One Who sustains and redeems us. As we offer praise to God, we are led to worship God our Creator, to praise Christ our Redeemer, and to be aware of the guidance of the Holy Spirit, our Comforter. In prayer, we praise God for Who He is.

Offering praise at the very beginning of worship is similar to greetings of deference at the human level. When we meet a prominent person, it is proper to acknowledge his or her position in society by addressing him or her in a particular way. We appropriately acknowledge persons who hold positions of authority in the State or Church by using designated titles to address them, such as Your Highness, His or Her Excellency, Sir, His Holiness, etc.

If we are so careful in addressing human leaders, who hold high earthly positions but are subject to human frailty and weaknesses, how much more must we be courteous as we approach the King of kings and Lord of lords!

Approach with Humility

The ancient Israelites were deeply conscious of the need for humility in approaching God. The awareness of the holiness of God caused them to enter His presence with humble, contrite hearts. Moses took off his shoes in the divine presence. Isaiah, seeing a vision of the Lord in His temple, trembled as he heard the cry, "Holy, holy, holy, is the Lord of hosts: the whole earth is full of his glory" (Isaiah 6:3).

The ancients knew what it was to be humble in the presence of God. If we are to "walk humbly with thy God" as the prophet exhorts us (Micah 6:8), then we must approach God in humility. We must offer to Him our allegiance and render Him the praise that is due Him as Creator and Sustainer of the universe.

Throughout the ages, prayer has been marked by a very strong element of praise in the opening phrases. As we read the prayers of the Puritans, we are impressed by the way in which they offered praise to God. The element of praise is also very strong in the prayers of such religious leaders as St. Francis of Assisi, St. Theresa, Martin Luther, and John Wesley.

Yes, our forefathers in the faith knew what it was to be humble in the presence of God. A strong element of praise characterized their prayers. It is not always so prominent in the prayers we offer today. Yet, if our prayer life is to be truly meaningful and effective, we must recapture something of this humility before God in our prayer. If we are able to attain this objective and enrich our prayer life, then we must "walk humbly with thy God" (Micah 6:8). We must approach God in an attitude of humility and offer our allegiance, rendering to the Divine One the praise that is due Him as Creator and Sustainer of the universe. We must take seriously this challenge: "O magnify the Lord with me, and let us exalt his name together" (Psalm 34:3).

Corporate Praise and Prayer

Moreover, because we love the company of others, the element of praise figures prominently in corporate worship. Indeed, when prayer is offered by or on behalf of a congregation, the element of praise most often predominates. Why? Because when we get together, we are inspired to praise God and acknowledge His greatness.

Let us reflect for a moment on Psalm 95, also known as the "Venite," which means "Come." This deeply inspiring song of praise, which has been used in worship for many centuries both in Israel and in the Church, begins with the invitation to worship:

O come, let us sing unto the Lord: let us make a joyful noise to the rock of our salvation. Let us come before his presence with thanksgiving, and make a joyful noise unto him with psalms (vs. 1,2).

This encouragement to praise is so inviting that the worshiper can hardly resist it. The person who enters into the spirit of this psalm cannot help but praise God. The psalm draws us into the presence of God, and we are thus led to praise the Lord quite naturally.

The psalm continues with an acknowledgment of the greatness of God:

For the Lord is a great God and a great King above all gods. In his hand are the deep places of the earth: the strength of the hills is his also (vs. 3,4).

Note the strong rejection of idolatry is this verse. God alone is worthy to be praised.

The ancient Hebrews feared the sea. The greatness of God the Creator reminds us that the sea is His. He made it, and His hands formed the dry land.

With all this in mind, Psalm 95 climaxes in this exhortation: "O come, let us worship and bow down: let us kneel before the Lord our maker" (vs. 6).

Here the praise of God naturally leads to prayer. As we accept the invitation to worship the Lord and acknowledge the greatness of God, we can only fall on our knees and enter into the praise of God. Yes, the praise of God leads us ultimately to fall upon our knees in prayer to our Maker. Truly, prayer is praise!

Praise is Uplifting

Praise lifts us out of ourselves, out of our concerns for our own failings and weaknesses, and points us toward God – the Source of our strength.

The praise of God, offered in the context of fervent prayer, is a very powerful antidote to depression and self-pity. So often we succumb to these negative emotions. When we feel lonely, when we have been hurt by someone else, when we have failed in some great undertaking, or when we fall ill, we must offer praise to God! Worship lifts us from the depths of depression to the heights of joy and ecstasy in the presence of the Lord.

Psalm 130 illustrates this elevating power of praise. The psalmist begins in a depressed frame of mind.

Out of the depths have I cried unto thee, O Lord. Lord, hear my voice: let thine ears be attentive to the voice of my supplications (vs. 1,2).

We don't know the cause of his downcast state of mind. He may have offended God and was deeply conscious of his sinful act, which had driven a wedge between himself and his Maker. Nevertheless, he remembered that God is merciful. Reflecting upon the forgiveness of God, he placed himself entirely at His disposal. Evidently, his prayer was answered. In the closing verses he proclaimed, "Let Israel hope in the Lord: for with the Lord there is mercy, and with him is plenteous redemption" (vs. 7).

The psalmist, who began this prayer in the depths of despair, completed it by exhorting others with a word of hope and praising God for His wonderful redemptive works. Praising God helped to lift him out of the depths.

We see a similar dynamic at work in several other psalms. A person goes to God in prayer with a dejected, deeply burdened spirit. In this state, he or she begins to reflect upon the ways in which God has demonstrated His redemptive action in human experience. Contemplating God's saving work leads the person to praise the Lord.

Psalm 22, which begins with the famous Cry of Dereliction ("My God, my God, why hast thou forsaken me?"), ends with the psalmist proclaiming, "My praise shall be of thee in the great congregation" (vs. 25). Psalm 57 also begins with a cry of anguish, "Be merciful unto me, O God" (vs. 1) and ends with worship. "Be thou exalted, O God, above the heavens: let thy glory be above all the earth" (vs. 11).

Are you burdened by the pains, problems, and trials of this transitory life? You may find yourself lifted out of the depths and released from bondage simply by entering into praise. God reveals clear answers to complex problems in prayer. He will relieve you of longstanding, bottled-up anxieties. He will lift the guilt and burden of sin, replacing it with the joy of forgiveness and reconciliation. Through prayer God heals the sicknesses that afflict the body, mind, and soul. In this sense, prayer may be truly described as therapeutic. It is precisely for this reason that the apostle James exhorts us:

> *Is one of you ill? He should send for the elders of the congregation to pray over him and anoint him with oil in the name of the Lord. The prayer offered in faith will save the sick man, the Lord will raise him from his bed, and any sins he may have committed will be forgiven. Therefore confess your sins to one another, and pray for one another, and then you will be healed. A good man's prayer is powerful and effective (James 5:14-16, NEB).*

Perhaps you are "down in the dumps." Even as you read these lines, you may be facing some serious problems in your life that threaten your physical, mental, and spiritual well being – crippling debts, a broken marriage, children who are estranged from you, problems on your job, the acute pain of the loss of a loved one, or the ravages of a debilitating disease. If so, *now* is the time to praise the Lord. Even though the circumstances of life may be difficult for you, you are exhorted to place these concerns before the Lord as you draw near to Him.

Yes, as you enter into the inner chamber of deep communion with God, you will be lifted out of the depths of despair and into the heights of joy and peace. This is the unique experience of those who dwell continually in the presence of the Lord.

Thou wilt shew me the path of life; in thy presence is fulness of joy; at thy right hand there are pleasures for evermore (Psalm 16:11).

Let us render praise to God continually in prayer that we may be lifted from anxiety to peacefulness, from despair to hope, from sickness to health, from fear to faith. Yes, from the "wages of sin," which is death, to the gift of God in Christ, which is eternal life.

Chapter 3

Prayer is Thanksgiving

Praise naturally leads to thanksgiving. It is very easy to understand why this is so. When we praise God, we think of the ways in which He has helped and strengthened us over the years.

Indeed, praise and thanksgiving are inextricably bound up with the other. This is why we tend to confuse them and to speak as if praise and thanksgiving are the same. They are related, but they are to be distinguished from each other if we are to grow in our devotional life. Let us reflect on the relationship between these two vitally important elements of prayer.

When we praise God, we acknowledge His greatness, His majesty, His holiness, and His power. Like Isaiah, who saw the Lord exalted in the temple, we are overcome by His holiness – that distinctive quality of the Godhead. The sense of God's holiness so overwhelms us that we can do nothing but burst forth in praise to the Almighty God of Creation. (See Isaiah 6.) This outpouring of praise, in response to the contemplation of divine sovereignty, can be seen in this great hymn of praise:

Praise to the Lord, the Almighty, the King of Creation;
O my soul, praise Him, for He is thy health and salvation;
All ye who hear, brothers and sisters, draw near.
Praise Him in glad adoration.[1]

When we consider what God has done for us, in us, and through us, we are led to thank Him. Or, to put it another way, praise comes first and thanksgiving follows. We praise God before we thank Him. But we thank Him because we can praise Him! Thanksgiving is a logical consequence to praise.

This close relationship between praise and thanksgiving is constantly brought out in the great hymns of praise of the Bible – the Psalms. Let's examine Psalm 100.

This psalm, which has been paraphrased and used as a hymn of praise in Christian worship, is essentially an invocation – a call to the congregation gathered to participate enthusiastically in the worship of God. It begins: "Make a joyful noise unto the Lord, all ye lands! Serve the Lord with gladness: come before His presence with singing" (vs. 1,2).

The basis for praise is to be found in the next verse: "Know ye that the Lord he is God: it is he that hath made us, and not we ourselves; we are his people, and the sheep of his pasture" (vs. 3).

Note how the elements of praise and thanksgiving are so skillfully woven together in the next verse: "Enter into his gates with thanksgiving, and into his courts with praise: be thankful unto him, and bless his name" (vs. 4).

This invocation is an invitation to the congregation to enter into the spirit of worship by offering praise and thanks to God. Who can read these verses without bursting forth into praise and offering thanks to God, the Holy One, the Bountiful Provider? No wonder it concludes with the proclamation: "For the Lord is good; his mercy is everlasting; and his truth endureth to all generations" (vs. 5).

Clearly, a very close link exists between praise and thanksgiving. Both are essential to meaningful, Christian worship, of which prayer is such an important aspect.

Why Be Thankful?

In thanksgiving, we list the ways in which God has been good to us and thank Him for His benefits to us. Biblical teaching and Church history constantly remind us to give thanks to God. Christians have received so many blessings that we can do nothing but express our gratitude. (Exodus 15; Deut. 6:4-9; 12:1-12; Psalm 9; 136; Col. 3:16,17; Rev. 7:12).

The importance of appreciating what God has done for us can be seen in one of the New Testament miracles of healing. Ten lepers asked Jesus to heal them. The Master sent them to the priests, and on their way they were cleansed from their dreaded disease. Amazingly, only one of them – a Samaritan – returned to thank Jesus for this miracle of healing. Jesus' response reveals His surprise at their lack of gratitude.

Jesus said: "Were not all ten cleansed? The other nine, where are they? Could none be found to come back and give praise to God except this foreigner?" (Luke 17:17,18, NEB).

Whether we pray for short periods or long hours each day, thanksgiving should form an extremely important part of our prayer life. Whether we find the mornings or evenings more convenient for prayer, and whatever our religious background, we must continually remember why we should offer thanks to God.

Why should we be grateful? Here is just a short list of reasons:

- Life and health
- The property that is entrusted to us
- Some success we have recently experienced
- Our family and friends
- The provision of food for our bodies
- Freedom to worship
- The fellowship we enjoy as members of the Body of Christ

- Employment
- Salvation in Jesus Christ
- The order, beauty, and constancy of nature

This list is very short indeed. No doubt you would have no difficulty doubling it!

Count Your Blessings

No matter how bad our situation might appear to be, no matter how many pains and frustrations we may bear, no matter how unfortunate our circumstances may be, we can still find something to thank God for. Why is this so important for us to remember? All too easily we can become complacent and take much for granted. Or we may sink into self-pity and think that our lot in life is worse than that of anyone else we know. We can be greatly helped in our Christian endeavor by reflecting on our daily experiences.

Many years ago a prominent layman told me that at the end of each day, he would tabulate his negative and positive experiences. With a twinkle in his eye, he testified, "You know, Reverend, the pluses always add up to more than the minuses. Always!"

Isn't this true of your life? Haven't you found that despite all the negative, difficult experiences you have had to face, the Lord has brought you through them? Indeed, haven't you discovered the profound truth in that old saying: "Count your blessings, name them one by one, and it will surprise you what the Lord has done!"

Years ago, while a student at theological college in Jamaica, I used to stay with a minister and his family during my holidays. He sometimes asked his little daughter to say grace. Inevitably, she would repeat this well known grace as we sat for our meal:

God is great.
God is good.
Let us thank Him for our food. Amen.

This little child's grace, as is so often the case with devotions designed for children, has a message that we all need to take to heart. It also helps us to appreciate both the close tie and the clear distinction between praise and thanksgiving. God is great, therefore, we must praise Him. God is good, therefore, we must thank Him.

Yes, we praise God because of Who He is: Holy, Creator, Sustainer. We thank God for what He has done and continues to do for us, in us, and through us. Indeed, praise and thanksgiving are different sides of the same coin – worship.

In the course of this transitory life, we will encounter trials and tribulations. We will face difficult situations. We know that "life is not a bed of roses." We will have problems in our homes and family life, in our marriages, in our finances, and even in our spiritual endeavor. Trials and temptations will test our faith. In such moments, we must remember the benefits we have received and "count our blessings."

Thankful in Adversity

The ancient Israelites, in their moments of despair, recalled their experiences of God's salvation in the Exodus and the great battles of deliverance as recorded in the Heilsgeschichte, their salvation history. Likewise, when we face difficulty, we should remember the ways God blessed us in the past. As we render thanks for them, we will find strength to continue our earthly endeavors. So shall we be enabled to offer praise and thanks to God even in the midst of adversity.

Through all the changing scenes of life,
In trouble and in joy,
The praises of my God shall still
My heart and tongue employ.

What can we say about the element of thanksgiving? It should form an integral part of our prayer. Moreover, our prayer should be filled with thanksgiving no matter what our situation in life. Offering thanks will greatly enrich our prayer life. More profoundly, our whole life should be characterized by an attitude of thankfulness.

When asked, "How are you?" a Christian gentleman inevitably responded with this thought-provoking answer: "Much to be thankful for!" He said this whether he was on top of the world or on his sick bed. What a superb example of the thankful attitude that should permeate the life of every Christian!

Since there is always something to thank God for, our lives should be characterized by a sense of gratitude to our Covenant God "who for us men and our salvation was made Man." Whatever our circumstances, no matter how bitter or painful our experiences, in the midst of our trials and tribulations, we should still demonstrate a thankful attitude toward God. The apostle Paul offers some very sound advice for us:

Let Christ's peace be arbiter in your hearts; . . . And be filled with gratitude. Let the message of Christ dwell among you in all its richness. Instruct and admonish each other with the utmost wisdom. Sing thankfully in your hearts to God, with psalms and hymns and spiritual songs. Whatever you are doing, whether you speak or act, do everything in the name of the Lord Jesus, giving thanks to God the Father through him (Col. 3:16,17, NEB).

Yes, prayer is thanksgiving.

Suggested Questions and Exercises

1   What is prayer?

2   Look at the list of definitions of prayer in chapter one. Which two would you select as being the most suitable?

3   Do you agree that prayer is the soul's sincere desire uttered or unexpressed?

4   Write a short prayer that includes the elements of praise and thanksgiving.

5   What is the difference between praise and thanksgiving in prayer?

6   In what ways would you like to see the prayer life of your church improve?

7   Prayerfully consider the possibility of starting a prayer group in your home.

8   Why is it true that "confession is good for the soul"?

Chapter 4

Prayer is Petition

The power of prayer is great indeed! Throughout the ages, people from all walks of life – saints and sinners, rich and poor, black and white, old and young – have all experienced the great spiritual power that comes through prayer.

Prayer unlocks the gates of heaven. In prayer we draw near to God with a humble, contrite heart. Yes, in prayer we ask Him for and about those things that we most earnestly desire. The Bible gives many illustrations of those who came to God with their request and received that for which they had prayed.

The Cry of the Barren

Hannah, one of the two wives of Elkanah, suffered for many years from the social disgrace of barrenness. Childless Hebrew women of her day were despised and subjected to several social pressures. Her anguish at not being able to bear children was compounded by the fact that her rival, Elkanah's "other wife," sarcastically jeered her.

Hannah entered the temple in this depressed state and prayed to God for the gift of a son. The Scriptures record the incident with these moving words:

So Hannah rose up after they had eaten in Shiloh, and after they had drunk. Now Eli the priest sat upon a seat by the post of the temple of the Lord. And she was in bitterness of soul, and prayed unto the Lord, and wept sore.

And she vowed a vow, and said, O Lord of hosts, if thou wilt indeed look on the affliction of thine handmaid, and remember me, and not forget thine handmaid, but wilt give unto thine handmaid a man child, then I will give him unto the Lord all the days of his life....

And it came to pass, as she continued praying before the Lord, that Eli marked her mouth. Now Hannah, she spake in her heart; only her lips moved, but her voice was not heard: therefore Eli thought she had been drunken.

And Eli said unto her, How long wilt thou be drunken? put away thy wine from thee.

And Hannah answered and said, No, my lord, I am a woman of a sorrowful spirit: I have drunk neither win nor strong drink, but have poured out my soul before the Lord (1 Samuel 1:9-15).

What an apt, moving description of the prayer of petition! In prayer, we draw near to God in the most intimate way and reveal to Him the depths of our hearts – our highest heights, our deepest hurts, our most intimate secrets, our deepest sorrows, and our greatest joys. Petition is pouring out our heart to the Lord.

The priest understood her situation. He bid her leave the temple and expressed his own desire that her prayer should be answered: "Go in peace: and the God of Israel grant thee thy petition" (1 Samuel 1:17).

And so, in the fullness of time, her prayer was answered and she had a son. In accord with her vow, she dedicated him to the Lord. That child grew to become one of the greatest religious leaders of all time – Samuel. No wonder! He was conceived as a result of prayer, nurtured in an atmosphere of prayer, and he himself was a man of prayer!

Hannah, a woman of faith, believed that God could and would answer prayer. She approached the Almighty in this confidence. In her persistence she received what she had requested.

Elements of Petition

The earnest pleading of Hannah for a son, a plea born out of deep anguish in very trying circumstances, highlights the essential nature of one of the most important elements of prayer – petition. This word, derived from the Latin word for "request," expresses something that is to be found in most of our prayers – the making of requests to God.

In Medieval times, when the monarchy had much more executive authority than at present, it was often used by the subject in making requests of their king or queen. Something of this element still survives in our understanding of the word, which is defined as "a formal request to a superior or one in authority for some favor, privilege, redress of a grievance, or the like!"[1] In the judicial system, this aspect is clear when an attorney "prays" for mercy on behalf of a client.

This aspect of prayer is so strong that it often prevails over all the others. Thus, if you were to ask some people, "What is prayer?" – especially those who do not have much of a religious background – their answer might be, "Asking God for things!" While those who are of a sensitive nature might not agree with such a pragmatic way of looking at prayer, humanly speaking, such an answer can hardly be too strongly contested. In prayer, we do make our needs known to God. In this sense, it is not too much to state that "prayer is petition." If this is so, what can we say about this element of prayer?

First, petition is the most natural and spontaneous aspect of prayer. When people find themselves in a most desperate situation – in a storm or shipwreck, in an accident, or deeply in debt – even those who claim not to be religious may turn to God in prayer as a last resort. We have heard stories of pilots, having engine trouble, who landed their plane "on a wing and a prayer!"

This universal element of prayer as petition, asking the Deity for help in most desperate situations, is evident in the Book of Jonah. Commanded to go to Nineveh in the east, the prophet fled from the presence of God and boarded a ship heading for Tarshish in the west! A terrible storm caused the boat to be cast to and fro upon the waves. The pagan sailors all prayed for safety to their gods. They also urged Jonah, scolding him, "Arise, call upon thy God!" (Jonah 1:6).

Even the most irreligious of persons, when things get tough, will turn to God in prayer. Petition, for the Christian, however, is based upon the conviction that God is good. In this respect, it is very closely related to thanksgiving.

When we give God thanks, we do so on the basis of the conviction that He is good and caring. By the same token, when we make our request known to Him in the context of petitions, we do so on the basis of the conviction that He is good and that He really cares for us.

Jesus Christ, who Himself was constantly in prayer to God, teaches us about God's heart for us. He reminds us of the goodness of God, our Heavenly Father who cares for us. In the Sermon on the Mount, He declares that the God who cares for the sparrows and the lilies of the field has a very special concern for mankind (Matthew 6:28-34). Again, in the treatise on prayer in Luke's Gospel, He notes that an earthly father has the wisdom and care to provide for the needs of his children (Luke 11:10-13). Since God is good, we can confidently approach Him and place before Him our needs, our deepest concerns, our greatest anxieties, and our deepest pains.

Trust in God is the very basis of petition. We approach God, trusting Him. We believe that He is good and will hear us.

Therefore, we can – and should – be bold in prayer. We must also be quite specific. When Hannah prayed to God, she made it abundantly clear that she wanted a son. She had been harassed by her rival, who daily ridiculed her because she had no child. She was ostracized by other women because she was barren. Indeed, there must have been those who implied, like the friends of Job, that she was in some way to blame for being cursed with barrenness! When she approached God, she did so boldly. She came with a particular request – a son. She was bold and she was specific.

Like Hannah, we should be bold and specific in our petitions. Vague prayers are not enough, especially when we approach an Almighty God Who cares for us!

What Should You Ask God For?

Because prayer is petition – pleading with God, seeking His intervention in our lives, asking for His guidance in decision-making – there is no limit to the concerns that we may bring before God in prayer. The list below, which is by no means exhaustive, includes some of these concerns:

1. Prayer for health and healing – We include prayers offered to combat illnesses that bring suffering to mankind. In our contemporary world, we think especially of those suffering from AIDS.

2. Prayer for prosperity and financial security – These are the concerns of people with regard to their financial condition with special prayers for deliverance from debt.

3. Happiness.

4. Success in examinations.

5. Fertility – Prayers by married couples who are childless and anxious for children. We may call these "Hannah prayers."

6. Prayer for a home.

7.   Prayer for a suitable life partner.

8.   Prayer for employment.

9.   Prayer for promotion on one's job.

10. Prayer to lose weight.

11. Prayer for safety on a journey – by land, sea, or air.

12. Prayer for self-control.

13. Prayer for moral guidance.

14. Prayer for spiritual growth – We may ask for deeper spirituality to overcome temptations and the wandering mind in prayer.

Persistence Pays Off

Moreover, the Bible clearly teaches that our prayer life should be marked by persistence and steadfastness. It is not enough to just pray once or twice and then dismiss prayer as "ineffective" when one's request is not granted. We must pray constantly and diligently. We must not give up easily in prayer.

Consider Hannah! She did not go to the temple at Shiloh and pray once. Rather, as she went to that holy place year by year, she poured out her heart in earnest prayer for a son. Indeed, if we examine the text carefully, we can conclude that she was a woman of prayer who spent hours each day on her knees.

Likewise, the great religious leaders of Israel were given much to prayer. Abraham, Moses, and the prophets were constantly in prayer. Elijah, by means of fervent prayer, wrought great victories for the Lord (1 Kings 17:19-24; 18:20-46).

As we examine the New Testament, we find Jesus constantly in prayer. It was His custom to begin the day in communion with His Heavenly Father. "And in the morning, rising up a great while before day, he went out, and departed into a solitary place, and there prayed" (Mark 1:35).

Jesus told parables to exhort His disciples to practice persistence in prayer. In the Parable of the Friend at Midnight (Luke 11:5-8), He told of a man who had nothing to offer a late night visitor. To avoid embarrassment, he went to the home of a friend and banged at the door until the friend arose and gave him bread. Jesus said it was not because of friendship that the man arose and gave him the loaf he needed; it was because of his persistence, or "importunity" as the King James Version puts it. The New English Bible brings out the lesson in language that is more relevant to us:

> *I tell you that even if he will not provide for him out of friendship, the very shamelessness of the request will make him get up and give him all he needs (Luke 11:8, NEB).*

Annoyed with the constant banging on his door, the man got up and gave his friend the loaf that he wanted. In this dramatic way Jesus drove home the importance of persistence in prayer. He also made the same point in an another parable in which a persistent widow wore down a harsh judge, forcing him to give in to her request (Luke 18:1-8).

Be Sincere

These virtues – boldness and persistence in prayer – are solidly based on a principle that is absolutely essential for effectiveness in petition: sincerity. This word implies purity, a lack of guile or anything that is deceptive. There is an important lesson for all of us! In our everyday living, and in our relationships with others, we often hesitate to reveal our true needs. We may find ourselves dying from hunger. When offered a meal, however, we may refuse it with a polite "No, thank you." We may want to impress others with our wealth by spending much while we are deeply in debt. We may even adopt double standards, appearing to live an upright life in one situation but being quite the opposite. No wonder Shakespeare so aptly observed: "All the world's a stage and all the men and women merely players!"[2]

He was right! So often in life we put on a show in order to impress others. When we come to God, however, none of this pretence is necessary! We can come to Him with our deepest needs. We can make our requests known to Him, confident that He will hear us.

This is precisely why we need to be bold and persistent in making our requests known to God. If we are in need of a job, let us ask Him to provide for us. We may need divine assistance in many ways. We may face problems in our marriage; we may be overweight; we may be deeply in debt. Whatever our condition, we can let God know, confident that He will hear us! Yes, it is true. "Thou art coming to a King, Great petitions with thee bring."[3]

As we close this chapter, let us return to Hannah's urgent request for a son. In her prayer, she demonstrated all the qualities that make for effectiveness in the prayer of petition – faith, boldness, persistence, and sincerity. She believed that the God of her fathers could and would answer prayer. In this confidence she approached God and received what she asked for.

And what about you, my dear friend? Are there great unfulfilled desires in your life? Do you have needs that seem to become greater with each passing day? Are you frustrated and about to give up because your prayers have not been answered? While your faith is being tested, you must hold on. Jesus promised, "Therefore I tell you, whatever you ask in prayer, believe that you receive it, and you will" (Mark 11:24, RSV). Pray confidently that the great and good God Who is the Creator, the God of Abraham, Isaac, and Jacob, will answer you and grant your petitions. Yes, like Hannah, you must be willing to pray without ceasing.

> *O what joy we often forfeit.*
> *O what needless pain we bear.*
> *All because we do not carry*
> *Everything to God in prayer.*[4]

A Mother Who Prayed

A young mother smiled as she held her firstborn in her arms just after giving birth. She had every reason to be proud of this bouncing baby boy! As she held her son and while her husband also beamed with joy, she quietly offered a special prayer to God. Like Hannah she prayed that her son would grow up to become a full-time servant of the Lord. And, like Mary, she kept this petition a secret for a long time.

Eventually, when the child grew up, he became conscious of a call from God. He responded and became a minister of the Gospel. It was not until after he had served for some years in the ministry that his mother revealed to him the content of her prayer at his birth.

In giving his testimony, this minister continues to encourage mothers to pray for their children at birth, to ask God to call their children into one of the many ministries of the Church.

Today, the leaders of many church bodies complain that there are not enough young people coming forward to serve as priests, ministers, and deacons. Indeed, the situation is serious in some churches with the average age of the clergy being well over fifty. There is an urgent need for young people "to fill the gaps."

Are you a young mother or father who has just experienced an addition to your family? Do not fail to constantly pray for your child. Yes, pray that he or she may grow up to be a faithful soldier of Christ. If more parents offered prayers at birth, dedicating their children to the service of the Lord, many more young people would offer themselves for the ministry of the Church!

Chapter 5

Prayer is Confession

"Confession is good for the soul!" This old adage contains a great truth. Confession, the acknowledging of sinfulness, is essential for our spiritual well being.

In this chapter we will ponder why confession is so necessary, examine its meaning, and discover ways in which confession can improve the effectiveness of our own prayer life and our relationships with God and man.

First of all, confession concerns our relationship to God. We live in relationship with others – our family, our friends, our employers, and the people that we meet in various situations. Our relationships to these people are very important to us as social beings. Our lives are deeply affected by these encounters with others. From the Christian perspective, the supreme relationship – that which governs all others – is our relationship with God.

The most important question a person can ask himself is, "How can I get right with God?" When we ask this question, we realize that we are not in right relationship with our Maker, that a gulf exists between God and ourselves.

What is the reason for this broken relationship with God? The answer is sin. Violating divine law causes a break in our relationship with God. As the late Professor Paul Tillich so often reminded us, sin is the cause of estrangement between God and man.

We commit deliberate sins when we knowingly transgress the law of God – when we steal, commit adultery, lie, or murder. Some of our sins, however, are committed unwittingly. These are sometimes known as "sins of omission." Whether they are done deliberately or inadvertently, they still violate the law of God. As Carl Menninger has demonstrated, such acts lead to a breaking of our relationship with God.

Admitting Our Guilt

When our relationship with God is marred, what can we do? If we want to see the relationship restored, we must first admit our guilt and take responsibility for what we have done. To put it bluntly, confession is essential because, in the words of the prophet Isaiah, "All we like sheep have gone astray; we have turned every one to his own way" (Isaiah 53:6).

It is never easy for anyone to admit guilt. A school boy once made a promise to help the members of his class with a project on a Saturday morning. When the day came, however, he decided to stay home. The following Monday his teacher rebuked him for not showing up as he had promised. The little boy felt very sorry and was made to apologize for it.

Because it is difficult to admit what we have done wrong, all too often we try to excuse ourselves and cover up our sins. So often we want to plead, like the man in court, "guilty with explanation." We excuse ourselves by laying the blame somewhere else. We blame our background, society, the Government, the Church, our friends – anyone but ourselves. Acting this way only proves that we truly are "children of Adam."

In the Fall, Adam and Eve sinned by disobedience. When God rebuked Adam for disobedience, he shirked the responsibility of admitting his own guilt. What was his excuse? Adam said he had been led into temptation by the woman God gave to him, who in turn, blamed it on the serpent! (Genesis 3:9-13) Talk about "passing the buck!"

No, it is not enough for us to blame others for our sins and mistakes. In most cases, we really should be looking at ourselves. When circumstances beyond our control are involved, we are not to be held responsible for our actions. But, in most cases, we are individually responsible for our sins.

In the days of the prophet Ezekiel, some blamed their ancestors for their situation. They excused themselves by repeating this proverb: "The fathers have eaten sour grapes, and the children's teeth are set on edge" (Ezekiel 18:2).

The prophet, however, would not allow them to continue to blame their sins on their ancestors! He taught the doctrine of individual responsibility. They should not blame their ancestors for their situation; they should acknowledge that their own sinful actions led to their predicament (Ezekiel 18:3-18).

We can learn much from these biblical incidents. Whenever we do something wrong, such as hurting someone's feelings, we sin. We should acknowledge our sins before God. This is the only way we will be able to return to a right relationship with Him. Yes, the admission of one's guilt is the first and most fundamental step in the process of confession.

If we say that we have no sin, we deceive ourselves, and the truth is not in us. If we confess our sins, he is faithful and just to forgive us our sins, and to cleanse us from all unrighteousness (1 John 1:8,9).

The purpose of confession, then, is to obtain the forgiveness of God, that we may be reconciled to Him. But confession has a deeper purpose! It is also for renewing us for further ministry and service to others.

When we study confession in prayer, we can learn a lot from the incident involving David and Bathsheba. In fact, this episode can be found in virtually every in-depth discussion of the subject of confession. David's great prayer of confession, as recorded in Psalm 51, models the right attitude and action. Let's look at the circumstances leading up to his cry for mercy.

King David had won great victories and had established Jerusalem as the capital of ancient Israel. Now in the later years of his reign, David no longer went out to war; instead he sent his generals to do the fighting. There is the root of his sin! He was idle. As we so often say, "The devil finds work for idle hands."

Walking around the roof of his palace at night, David saw a beautiful lady bathing and he was attracted. He found out that she was Bathsheba, the wife of Uriah the Hittite. He brought her to the palace, and she became pregnant as a result of their tryst. Then David invited Uriah home from the battlefield, thinking he would lie with his wife. When Uriah refused out of loyalty to his comrades, David arranged for him to be placed in a dangerous position on the battlefield where he was killed!

The duplicity and wickedness of the king stand in stark contrast to the sincerity and simple honesty of Uriah who, in utter loyalty to the king, refused to go to his own home! After Uriah's death, David took Bathsheba to be his wife.

But that was not the end of the story. The Bible says, "But the thing that David had done displeased the Lord" (2 Samuel 11:27). The king had committed both adultery and murder – clear violations of the ancient covenant law of Israel. The Lord, the Righteous and Holy One, could not allow such blatant violation of the divine law to go unchecked, even if the king had perpetrated it!

God sent the prophet Nathan to sternly rebuke the king for his action. In a vivid parable, he portrayed a rich man who had viciously robbed a poor man of his meager possession. Responsible for executing justice in Israel, David flatly condemned the man. Then the prophet dramatically turned upon him and charged, "Thou art the man!"

What did the king do when confronted with his action? Did he exercise his power and snub the advice of the prophet? Did he try to excuse his actions? Did he claim, "As king I'll do as I please"? No! He didn't resort to any of these tactics.

In an act of supreme contrition, he confessed his sin to God. Psalm 51 records the heartfelt cry of David. This excellent prayer of confession teaches us how to approach God after being convicted of our sin.

Psalm 51 can be divided into the following sections:

Verses 1-2	Cry for mercy
Verses 3-6	Act of confession
Verses 7-9	Prayer for cleansing (reconciliation)
Verses 10-17	Prayer for restoration

A Cry for Mercy

This great prayer of confession begins appropriately with a cry for mercy. David appeals to God on the basis of His covenant love, which had been demonstrated in so many ways in his own relationship to God. He begins:

Have mercy upon me, O God, according to thy lovingkindness: according unto the multitude of thy tender mercies blot out my transgressions (vs. 1).

Knowing the mercy and lovingkindness of God, David appealed to God on these grounds. Remember that God's love was supremely manifested in sending Jesus Christ to be our Savior. Thus, we have all the more reason to appeal to the mercy of God.

Act of Confession

The penitent David, having cried out to the Lord for mercy, rapidly moves to the essential matter of his prayer – the confession of his sin. In the presence of God, like Isaiah in the temple (Isaiah 6:5), he is deeply aware of his sinful condition. In this most contrite frame of mind, he humbly confesses with sorrow:

For I acknowledge my transgressions: and my sin is ever before me (vs. 3).

"I acknowledge my sin!" How utterly important that we admit our sin. The psalmist, unlike Adam and Eve, does not shift the blame to anyone else or excuse his wicked deed. He admits that he has done wrong. This reveals the very heart of confession – the admission of guilt, the willingness of an individual or corporate body to take responsibility for violating the divine law. This is the first step to restoring one's relationship to God after it has been breached by sin.

The psalmist, in his highly penitential mood, continues:

Against thee, thee only, have I sinned, and done this evil in thy sight (vs. 4).

The psalmist's confession conveys a profound theological truth – sin is first and foremost against God. Yes, David's act of adultery was also committed against Uriah, the husband of Bathsheba. But Scripture clearly tells us that David and his household suffered precisely because his sin was against God. By committing adultery and murdering this man, the king had violated two of the most fundamental precepts of the covenant. Yes, the king, who was expected to be the champion of Yahweh's justice, had himself committed an act of grave injustice!

David's violation of divine law resulted in a series of terrible judgments upon his house. The child, who was conceived as a result of the king's adulterous act, died just a few days after birth. The royal family was plagued with instability and an act of incest. The king's favorite son led a rebellion that almost succeeded in dethroning him. These events, known as "The Succession Narrative," all came as a result of David's sin.

This narrative describes one clear lesson – God does not tolerate sin! Throughout the Bible this principle is repeated again and again. No one can thoughtfully read the Bible without realizing that it is impossible to get away with sin. Scripture warns us, "Be sure your sin will find you out" (Numbers 32:23). Sin is not primarily the violation of human laws. It is first and foremost the violation of divine law. Sin is not primarily against our neighbor or society; it is against God.

It is precisely for this reason that the first four of the Ten Commandments focus on our relationship to God, which is the supreme relationship, and the others (the second table) focus on our relationship to others. Because we are created in the divine image, our first responsibility is to obey God. Moreover, God has commanded us to be in a right relationship with Him by being in a harmonious relationship with our neighbor. When we steal, commit adultery, lie, or cheat, we offend not only our neighbor, we offend God. Sin, in the final analysis, is always against God! This is why our Lord summed up the Ten Commandments with these words:

Thou shalt love the Lord thy God with all thy heart, and with all thy soul, and with all thy mind, and with all thy strength: this is the first commandment. And the second is like, namely this, Thou shalt love thy neighbour as thyself. There is none other commandment greater than these (Mark 12:30,31).

When we sin against our brother in any way whatsoever – gossip, cheating, stealing, violating his or her rights – we sin against God. As David said, "Against thee, thee only, have I sinned, and done this evil in thy sight" (vs. 4).

Prayer for Cleansing

After having humbly admitted his guilt, David petitions the God of mercy for cleansing. This prayer marks a major advance in his spiritual development. He is prepared not only to admit that he has done wrong, but also to be cleansed from his sin that he might grow spiritually. To put it more pointedly, he asks for cleansing in order that he might not commit the same sin again.

Thus he prays, "Create in me a clean heart, O God; and renew a right spirit within me" (vs. 10).

Confession is both negative and positive. Negatively, it calls for the admission of guilt, of being willing to acknowledge that one has done that which displeases God. Positively, it leads to cleansing from those thoughts and words that lead to destructive actions.

More profoundly, confession is a therapeutic process that heals the soul. Just as poison in an infected wound must be drained away before healing can take place, so the soul must be purged of evil inclinations in order for the healing, brought about by confession, to take effect.

Prayer for Restoration

David's prayer for cleansing expressed his desire for the forgiveness of God and reconciliation. He acknowledged that his sin created a breach between God and himself. This sense of estrangement from God is the source of his sorrow. He desires to get back into a right relationship with His Maker.

David, who had once enjoyed deep fellowship with God, now finds himself far from God. In confession he seeks to be restored to God, and so he prays, "Cast me not away from thy presence" (vs. 11). What a prayer! Every child of God should passionately desire to dwell continually in His presence!

The element of confession runs through this psalm very much like the theme in a great musical symphony. Again and again, the psalmist admits his guilt and prays for the strength to amend his ways and to be reconciled to God. His consuming desire, however, is to engage in the praise of God. So, he cries: "O Lord, open thou my lips; and my mouth shall shew forth thy praise" (vs. 15).

Why does the psalmist make this request? Why does he express the desire to praise the Lord? As we seek to answer these questions, we realize the essential relationship between confession and praise in the process of prayer to Almighty God.

While conscious of his sin and the resulting estrangement from God, David was deeply disturbed in spirit that he was unable to do what he desired most – to praise the Lord. But having confessed his sin and having been reconciled to God, he can burst forth into praise.

The example of David, "a man after God's own heart," shows us how to practice confession in our prayers. When we have broken the divine law, let us go to God and confess our sins. It does us no good to cover up our sins. We do not go to God to inform Him of our sins. God already knows that we have transgressed. The omniscient Deity knows even before we come to Him that we have sinned! Let us, therefore, get it right.

We do not tell God anything new when we confess our sins to Him. We admit to God that we have done wrong, taking responsibility for our actions. The well-known story of George Washington confessing that he had cut down a cherry tree is useful here. His father probably knew that he had done so. The important thing is that the boy "owned up" to having done this bad deed.

The willingness to take responsibility for our sinful actions leads to cleansing and opens up the way for us to receive the forgiveness of God. It is precisely when this is realized that the greatness of David comes into sharp relief. Some may ask, "How can David be considered a man after God's own heart when he abused his power by committing adultery and murdering the woman's husband?" David can be considered in this righteous manner because he had the guts to admit his guilt before God and the humility to seek divine forgiveness!

The path to perfection in the Christian life is not so much a continual advance to holiness as much as it is a slow process with advances and set backs. The person needs to have a willingness to admit his or her faults, "pick up the pieces," and move on to greater achievements! So often it really means "Climbing up new calvaries ever ..."

It is, therefore, very significant that this great prayer of confession concludes: "The sacrifices of God are a broken spirit: a broken and a contrite heart, O God, thou wilt not despise" (vs. 17).

These words, written at a time when sacrifices were offered to seek reconciliation with God, assures us that what the Lord desires is a "contrite heart." God, in His divine mercy, will receive and forgive the sinner who approaches Him humbly, confesses his guilt, and seeks divine pardon. Indeed, isn't this assurance at the very heart of the Gospel?

If one theme runs throughout the Bible, it is this – God is love! Out of His love for erring, rebellious mankind, God sent His Son into the world. This is why the apostle Paul could say, "God was in Christ, reconciling the world unto himself" (2 Cor. 5:19). John proclaimed the essence of this Christian revelation in these immortal, challenging words:

For God so loved the world, that he gave his only begotten Son, that whosoever believeth in him should not perish, but have everlasting life (John 3:16).

Thus men and women in all ages and from all walks of life have turned to God in penitence, confessing their sins and experiencing the joy of forgiveness and reconciliation. Despite their sin, they have been ransomed, healed, and restored. Forgiven by God, they continue their spiritual journeys, ever trusting in the God of their salvation.

What about you? Are you burdened by sin? Do your past sins still trouble your conscience? Do you feel hindered from making spiritual progress? Is your relationship with God marred by sin? Do you have a burning desire to be reconciled to your Maker?

The message of this chapter is for you! If you approach God, offering the prayer of confession, acknowledging your sinfulness, and seeking His forgiveness, then you too will receive divine forgiveness. You too will be reconciled to God. You will be forgiven and reconciled to God – the God Who was in Christ reconciling the world to Himself. Come then, my brothers and sisters, and with a humble, contrite heart, confess your sins to God.

Let us therefore come boldly unto the throne of grace, that we may obtain mercy, and find grace to help in time of need (Hebrews 4:16).

Confession is utterly essential for spiritual growth! When we acknowledge past sins, we receive present forgiveness and are endowed with renewed strength for future spiritual warfare. Sincere prayer almost always involves a strong element of confession. Yes, confession is good for the soul! It is also good for the body, mind, and spirit.

Jesus is seeking the wanderers
Yet, why do they roam?
Love only waits to forgive and forget:
Home! Weary wanderer, home!
Wonderful love dwells in the heart of the Father above.
Robert Walmsley

Exercises

1 What is confession?

2 Why is confession so necessary in prayer?

3 How can we improve our prayer life by the effective use of confession?

4 Think of a sin you have committed recently. Write a short prayer of confession seeking God's forgiveness.

5 Discuss this statement: In confession we do not tell God anything about ourselves. We acknowledge to Him what we have done.

Chapter 6

Prayer is Intercession

Samuel was displeased with the Israelites! This great man of God, who had been the judge – the spiritual and administrative leader of Israel for nearly forty years – was now faced with a major crisis of confidence! The Israelites came to him and asked for a king. Samuel found it hard to agree with this request on two grounds: one theological, the other personal.

Theologically, he held to the concept of the Kingship of God. He believed that there was no King of Israel other than Yahweh. This concept of kingship contrasted sharply to that which was held by the other nations of ancient times.

The kings of these pagan nations were despots who ruled with an iron hand. Samuel was not happy with the prospect of such a monarch ruling in the land of God. Samuel believed that the Lord alone was the King; the earthly ruler was merely "the Lord's executor." The earthly monarch was there only to carry out the will of God and not to exercise power over his subjects.

Samuel also regarded this as a personal slight. The Israelites were quite satisfied with his tenure as their administrative and spiritual ruler, exercising power as delegated by God. But his sons were not of the same spiritual caliber as their father, and the Israelites were worried about what might happen if they were called to exercise leadership. So, in a not-so-veiled criticism of the house of Samuel, they alleged that Samuel himself was becoming too old for the job and his sons were simply too corrupt to assume leadership (1 Samuel 8:4,5).

It must have been a bitter pill for the old man to swallow. In asking for a king, the Israelites not only rejected the concept of God as the only King of Israel but also rejected Samuel and his household!

What did Samuel do? His wise, compassionate response showed that he was indeed a man of God. He did not agree with their request. He must have felt very downcast and saddened. Despite this, he made just one promise to them.

In an act of supreme graciousness, this old man said, "As for me, God forbid that I should sin against the Lord in ceasing to pray for you" (1 Samuel 12:23).

Samuel's response is exemplary. Although the Israelites had rejected his advice and had criticized his sons, he still made it a point to pray for them. Indeed, in acting this way he foreshadowed the advice of the Master, "Pray for them which despitefully use you" (Matthew 5:44).

So far we have examined those aspects of prayer that concern our relationship with God. Since prayer is essentially communion with God, it is only natural that we should bring our concerns to God. This is why we offer God our praise and thanksgiving – and our confessions.

But there is another very important aspect of prayer – our concern for others. Our prayers should always contain an element of this concern for others. Today there is more appreciation of the importance of intercession in prayer. Indeed, as our world becomes more and more of a global village, we are made increasingly aware of the need of others and our responsibility to pray for them.

The Importance of Intercession

It is at once a great privilege and a major responsibility for Christians to pray for others. It is a privilege because those who need prayer want us to pray for them. Whether it be in the hospital ward, in an emergency of some kind, or in a dangerous situation such as being in an airplane with engine trouble, people often welcome your offer to pray. You probably know those who don't go to church but who say, "Pray for me!"

Often we agree to pray but soon forget their request. We must take these opportunities seriously! We should remember them when we offer prayer during our worship service, counting it a joy to be able to pray for others. The person who hardly ever darkens the door of a church, or even one who claims to be an atheist, appreciates a word of prayer when facing a major crisis in life – sickness, the loss of a loved one, or pending danger.

Perhaps you have heard the story of the man who had a family of four, including his wife and two children. Each evening he would pray: "God bless us four, no more!"

We may smile when we hear about this selfish gentleman who cared for only his family. So often our prayers are similar to his – very self-centered and limited to our family and circle of friends. This, however, is not in keeping with the nature of the Christian faith that we profess. As Christians, our prayer should never be selfish or self-centered. Rather, they should reflect our concern for the welfare of others.

When we reflect on our faith, we can conclude that offering intercessory prayer is our responsibility, something that naturally flows from our existence as members of the Body of Christ. How do we know what to pray in distressing situations? God Himself has promised to help us with this task.

Likewise the Spirit also helpeth our infirmities: for we know not what we should pray for as we ought: but the Spirit itself maketh

*intercession for us with groanings which cannot be uttered. And he
that searcheth the hearts knoweth what is the mind of the Spirit,
because he maketh intercession for the saints according to the will of
God (Romans 8:26,27).*

With the Holy Spirit personally assisting us, we should be encouraged to intercede for others more often.

The Corporate Nature of Humanity

The biblical teaching about mankind is based upon the concept
of its essentially corporate nature. This is expressed in God's comment regarding Adam's condition before the creation of Eve. "It is
not good that the man should be alone" (Genesis 2:18). The Bible
shows us that no one can realize his or her true potential apart
from the tribe or group to which he or she belongs. Thus, in the
patriarchal narratives, especially those about Jacob and Esau and
Joseph, the individual has identity and purpose only as part of the
tribal grouping. The action of the one, then, is bound up with the
destiny of the whole tribe and vice versa! For example, the terrible
sin of Achan brought calamity upon the whole nation (Joshua 7:1-
26).

The corporate nature of humanity developed fully in the history of Israel during the monarchy. A good king, one who obeyed
the teaching of Yahweh, brought blessings and prosperity upon
his people. A bad king, who "caused Israel to sin," brought disaster and defeat upon his people. The historical books, such as Kings
and Chronicles, are based upon this concept of the corporate nature of humanity in which the destinies of monarchs and their subjects are entirely bound up with each other.

Turning to the New Testament, this concept is developed in
teaching about the Church. The apostle Paul taught that the Church
is the Body of Christ, and that the individual members make up
this body. Because their lives touch each other, Christians are called
upon to care for each other. The apostle Paul concludes his exhortation on the Church by declaring, "All of you, then, are Christ's

body, and each one is a part of it" (1 Cor. 12:27, GNB). As a member of the Body of Christ, the Christian has a deep and special relationship to others who belong to Christ. As such, we should continually offer prayer for those who belong to "the household of faith" (Galatians 6:10).

What Motivates You to Pray?

Our prayers of intercession should not be limited to those who are members of the Church. Rather, they should be offered for all who are in need, whatever their color, race, condition, or creed. We need only reflect upon the ministry of our Lord Himself in order to realize how we must be concerned for the welfare of others.

The motivating force for our prayers of intercession must be love; not the fickle sentiment that is based upon emotion but genuine love, *agape*, which is essentially a concern for the well being of others. The Bible has a lot to say about this special kind of love.

Indeed, divine love is at the heart of the Gospel message. The Bible teaches that God is love. Its essential message is summed up by the apostle John in these immortal words:

For God so loved the world that he gave his only Son, that whoever believes in him should not perish but have eternal life (John 3:16, RSV).

The ministry of God's Son, Who came into the world to save sinners, was marked by deep concern for the welfare of all, especially the outcasts of society, including tax collectors, sinners, and beggars. Jesus Christ defined His ministry at its outset:

The Spirit of the Lord is upon me, because he has anointed me to preach good news to the poor. He has sent me to proclaim release to the captives and recovering of sight to the blind, to set at liberty those who are oppressed, to proclaim the acceptable year of the Lord (Luke 4:18,19 RSV).

Throughout His ministry Jesus demonstrated great concern for the welfare of others. He healed the sick, gave sight to the blind, fed the hungry multitudes, and even raised the dead.

In His prayers, Jesus remembered those who were His disciples and who would come to believe in Him in ages to come (John 17). In His sacrificial death upon the Cross, He was "numbered among the transgressors" (Isaiah 53:12), although He Himself committed no sin. By means of His death and resurrection, He wrought victory over sin and death for all who believed on Him. Truly, He can be described as "the man for others."

Since the Master cared so much for others, then we who are His disciples also ought to show love for those whom we meet. "This is the way the Master went, must not His servants tread the same?"

Our Master was quite explicit in our responsibility to others. He summed up the teaching of the law and the prophets by giving two great commandments:

Thou shalt love the Lord thy God with all thy heart, and with all thy soul, and with all thy strength, and with all thy mind; and thy neighbour as thyself (Luke 10:27).

The first of these commandments focuses on our relationship to God, which is the supreme relationship that governs all others. The first commandment is the basis of the aspects of prayer we have discussed thus far – praise, thanksgiving, petition, and confession. In offering praise to God, in making our petitions to God, in thanking God for benefits to us, and in making confession to God, we are praying in accord with the commandment to love God with the utmost integrity.

The second commandment focuses on our relationship to our neighbor – those we meet day by day. The Master commands us to love them as well. The biblical understanding of love is profound, calling upon us to exercise a genuine concern for the welfare of others. When we pray for those who are in need, when we intercede for sinners, the sick, and the bereaved, we pray in accord with the second great commandment of the Master. This commandment gives theological backing for offering prayers of intercession.

There is a very sound biblical and theological sanction for praying for others. This three-fold basis for the prayer of intercession – the corporate nature of humanity, the vicarious nature of the ministry of the Master, and the divine law of love – makes it obligatory for Christians to include prayers for others in virtually all devotional exercises. What qualities make for effective prayers of intercession?

Sympathy and Identification

It requires a great degree of sympathy and identification to be able to offer prayers that will really meet the needs of others. Just as our Father in heaven is sensitive to our needs, so we must be sensitive to the needs of others to offer the prayers that are most appropriate for them. Scripture gives us many examples of this.

Think about the call of Isaiah in the temple. This passage begins with an acknowledgment of the power, majesty, and holiness of God. Isaiah has a vision of the Lord "high and lifted up" as the seraphim proclaim, "Holy, holy, holy, is the Lord of hosts: the whole earth is full of his glory" (Isaiah 6:3).

The prophet's awareness of God's holiness make him conscious of his own sinful condition. But he is not alone. Rather, he becomes aware of the corporate nature of sin and identified with the nation.

Woe is me! for I am undone; because I am a man of unclean lips, and I dwell in the midst of a people of unclean lips: for mine eyes have seen the King, the Lord of hosts (Isaiah 6:5).

The prophet does not set himself apart from the sinful nation, but is deeply aware that he shares in its sinful condition. If we are to offer effective prayers of intercession, we cannot set ourselves apart from society. We must be painfully aware of its failure and shortcomings. Only in this way can we offer prayers that are relevant to its needs.

We must constantly think about the ways in which others may be tempted to sin, and pray for them. Job prayed for his children just in case they might have sinned. Job didn't wait until his children had done something wrong to pray for them. He prayed for them continually so they might be able to resist sin when tempted (Job 1:5). He was a father who was deeply sensitive to the needs of his children!

Sensitivity

God requires sensitivity from all of us. We must always be alert to even the unspoken needs of others so we can offer prayer and help in their time of need.

A minister was doing his pastoral rounds in the hospital one evening. As he was leaving, having visited a number of patients, he saw two ladies standing outside with deeply concerned expressions. He asked why they were so troubled. They explained that a gentleman who was very near and dear to them had become very ill. He was the husband of the older lady and the father of the younger one, her daughter.

The pastor visited the gentleman and had a word of prayer with him. Because this pastor was alert and noticed their concern, he had the opportunity to minister to a very sick man who needed prayer. His wife and daughter were most appreciative for his kindness!

Like this man, we must be alert even to the unspoken needs of others. Like the Master Himself, as we are sensitive to the plight of our neighbor, we will be able to effectively intercede (Mark 6:34, John 17).

Responsibility

Because it is our Christian duty to pray for others, we should do so whether they appreciate it or not. We should be persistent in offering prayer for them and continue to do so as long as we consider it necessary. This should depend not on whether they are receptive to us, but on our sense of responsibility for them before God.

Let's look at one of the great prayers of intercession – the prayer of Abraham for the cities of Sodom and Gomorrah. The inhabitants of these cities were very wicked. Yet, in a strange way, their destinies are bound up with that of Abraham, whose righteousness and loyalty to God stand in stark contrast to their sinfulness. Abraham's nephew Lot had chosen to dwell among the people of these cities – and their destruction was imminent!

Abraham prayed for these cities from a hill overlooking them. Several men from the city had spoken to the patriarch. As they were about to return to these wicked places, the Lord revealed to Abraham that He was about to destroy them. Here on the mount, overlooking the plains where Sodom and Gomorrah have sinned, Abraham began to pray for their salvation. With great compassion and persistence he asked the Lord to spare the people of these cities.

What a moving scene! A righteous man prayed for the salvation of two wicked cities. Like every true child of God, he took no pleasure in the death of sinners. Even as the outcry of the sins of the people rose to the heavens, the prayers of righteous Abraham rose to heaven pleading for mercy upon its erring inhabitants.

And Abraham drew near him [God] and said, "Wilt thou really sweep away the good and bad together? Suppose there are fifty good men in the city; wilt thou really sweep it away, and not pardon the place because of the fifty good men? Far be it from thee to do this – to kill good and bad together; for then the good would suffer with the bad. Far be it from thee. Shall not the judge of all the earth do what is just?" (Genesis 18:23-25, NEB).

Abraham continued to plead for these cities. His persistent intercession gradually led to a reduction of the number of innocent people required to save them. Finally, he made one last request.

Abraham said, "I pray thee not to be angry, O Lord, if I speak just once more: suppose ten can be found there?" He said, "For the sake of the ten I will not destroy it." When the Lord had finished talking with Abraham, he left him, and Abraham returned home (Genesis 18:32,33, NEB).

Here we see a great man of God pleading before the throne of mercy for people who were corrupt to the core. Eventually, the cities were destroyed because not even ten innocent people were found in them. But it was not for want of intercession. They must have been very wicked cities if so few righteous people could be found!

Pray for Them Anyway

The evil inhabitants of these two cities did not ask Abraham to pray for them! In fact, they were so depraved that they had forgotten God and abandoned any effort to conform to His moral law. It did not matter to them whether Abraham prayed for them or not!

Abraham offered persistent prayer for people who either could not or cared not to pray for themselves. This is the essence of intercession – a concern for others that is not based on our relationship to them but our understanding of their need. While the prayer of intercession is based on our relationship to others, our relationship to God ultimately controls the way in which we pray for others.

The wicked inhabitants of Sodom and Gomorrah had reached such depravity that it mattered not whether prayer was offered for them or not. Still Abraham prayed for them.

When we sense that people are in need of prayer, when we see that they're going the wrong way – even when they make it clear that they do not need or want us to pray – we should still continue to pray for them! It is not for us to determine whether people appreciate our prayers or even to wonder whether they want us to pray for them.

What is important is our relationship to God. If people are in need of prayer, even if they might not want prayer, we should still intercede for them because the Master has commanded us to do so. Our relationship to God, in the final analysis, determines whether we ought to pray for others. We cannot rely on our attitude or our relationship to them to guide us.

Don't worry about whether others want us to pray for them. If they are in need of God's intervention, go ahead and pray for them! Let God judge whether our prayers for them are in vain or whether they deserve the prayers offered on their behalf. Let us follow the example of Samuel who promised to pray for those who had rejected him. "As for me, God forbid that I should sin against the Lord in ceasing to pray for you" (1 Samuel 12:23).

Jesus in Gethsemane

Let's consider the greatest prayer of intercession of all time – the prayer of Jesus in the Garden of Gethsemane. Known to many scholars as "The Prayer of the Great High Priest," it is the longest prayer in the New Testament. In this solitary place, the Master entered into deep communion with God. John, "the beloved disciple," gave us an intimate glimpse of the Master at prayer. His account allows us to enter into "the holy of holies" and see the heart of Christ as He prayed for His disciples, the Church, and the world. Jesus suffered deep spiritual agony as He offered this powerful, comprehensive prayer of intercession. This prayer falls naturally into these distinct parts:

1. *Jesus' Relationship to God (vs. 1-5).*
2. *Jesus' Prayer for His disciples (vs. 6-19).*
3. *Jesus' Prayer for the Church and the World (vs. 20-26).*

1. Jesus' relationship to God (vs. 1-5). Jesus addressed God in that special way – "Father." He used the expression that a child of His time would instinctively speak to his or her earthly father. Jesus also taught His disciples to make their own petitions by beginning, "Our Father. . ." Jesus prayed that as He completed His mission on earth, He would be glorified. His mission provided the way for all mankind to enjoy eternal life.

How did He define eternal life? "This is eternal life: to know thee who alone art truly God, and Jesus Christ whom thou has sent" (John 17:3, NEB).

Jesus began with an invocation that placed His relationship to God in true perspective. In the context of this unique relationship, He expressed satisfaction that His ministry had lined up with the will of His Heavenly Father to grant eternal life to all who believe in Him.

2. Jesus' prayer for His disciples (vs. 6-19). Jesus prayed specifically for those whom God had given Him. Having called His disciples out of the world, Jesus knew they would continue His ministry by preaching, teaching, and healing the sick (Mark 3:13-15, Luke 9:1-6). They had been with Him throughout His ministry. Now, in the hour of persecution, they were especially in need of prayer.

Even as Jesus was praying, one disciple was plotting to betray Him to the religious authorities (John 18:1-9). Soon one of His most outspoken followers, Simon Peter, would deny that he ever knew Him (Matthew 26:69-75). When the soldiers came to arrest Jesus, all the disciples forsook Him and fled. In this crucial hour in which He was betrayed, His disciples were in special need of prayer.

3. Jesus' prayer for the Church (vs. 6-28). Even though the disciples failed the Master in this time of great testing, Jesus expressed great confidence in them. He believed that their ministry would bear fruit. He prayed confidently, "But it is not for these alone that I pray, but for those also who through their words put their faith in me" (John 17:20, NEB).

Peering down through the centuries, Jesus prophetically prayed for the Church in all ages. He prayed that those who would believe on Him would be united in their witness to the world. Ultimately, the mission of Christ and His Church, in all ages, was one and the same – bringing salvation to all mankind.

Our Model for Intercession

Jesus' example gives us a model to follow when we pray for others. How should we pattern our prayers of intercession?

First, we should get our relationship with God in proper perspective. Praise, petitions to God, confession, and thanksgiving for God's gifts to us should take place before intercession. We cannot pray effectively for others unless we first enter into a right relationship with God. This is precisely why the Bible declares, "The effectual fervent prayer of a righteous man availeth much" (James 5:16).

Here we have a striking parallel to our own witness as Christians. The Christian must first receive the saving grace of God in Christ before he or she can witness to others. John Wesley was not able to witness effectively to the world until he had his own conversion experience in which he testified, "I felt my heart strangely warmed." Similarly, we must first receive a right relationship with God in prayer before we can pray effectively for others.

Second, we remember before God those who are nearest and dearest to us. We pray for the members of our household – our parents, wives, children, and any others who are with us. We think of those who are members of our family and who are away from home – a child at school, a relative on vacation, a member of the family who is in the hospital. Next, we pray specifically for sick family members, and we think of relatives and friends who may have concerns. We should think especially of any elderly members of our family who are in a hospital or nursing home.

Third, we think of the household of faith – the Church. Jesus prayed for His disciples, those like us who seek to follow Christ. Let us remember the members of our local church. Many of our churches have weekly bulletins that list the members who are ill, abroad, or in any special need. Use this bulletin regularly as a means of praying for those in need.

Then we should bring before God the needs of our pastor. We often ask him to pray for us, but do we pray for him? Your pastor, as he goes about his duties, needs your prayer. Every pastor will testify that he is greatly assisted and encouraged in his ministry by knowing that members of the congregation remember him in their prayers.

Finally, having prayed for the Church, we should extend our prayer concerns to the wider community. We should pray for the nation in which we live and especially remember its leaders, both political and spiritual. The words of the apostle Paul to Timothy teach us how to pray for this specific need:

First of all, then, I urge that petitions, prayers, intercessions, and thanksgivings be offered for all men; for sovereigns and all in high office, that we may lead a tranquil and quiet life in full observance of religion and high standards of morality. Such prayer is right, and approved by God our Saviour, whose will it is that all men should find salvation and come to know the truth (1 Tim. 2:1-4, NEB).

We should be aware of the major concerns of those who are in authority in our nation. Our prayers of intercession would be greatly enriched as we keep abreast of current events that appear in our daily newspaper.

We should also pray for the whole community of mankind. We should be especially aware of the mission of the Church to the world. We can pray for the world, confident that in the end Christ will triumph over the forces of evil.

Intercession Requires Compassion

If we are to pray effectively for others, we must exercise compassion. Compassion leads to action for the welfare of others; it is not just "feeling sorry for them." It means being identified with them and, as a result, doing something concrete to improve their situation.

As we examine the ministry of the Master, we can see the meaning of compassion. When the multitudes came to Him in a desert place, they were hungry. The Master had compassion upon them because He knew their condition. This led Him to miraculously feed the multitudes. His compassion and prayer resulted in action that provided bread for their needs.

Likewise, as we intercede for others, we are led to do something positive to relieve their condition. Many testify that as a result of praying for a person with a particular need, they were moved to do something to help that person! Perhaps we can all think of times when our praying for someone moved us to action. Prayer ushers in action. In a profound sense intercession forms the link between "the world of work" and the "world of prayer." Intercession is comprehensive in nature. In intercession we join with the Lord in prayer for the benefit of another.

Including intercession adds variety, freshness, and vigor to our prayer life! As we begin to reflect upon the needs of our family, the Church, and the world, we soon realize that there is no end to the number of concerns that we can bring before the throne of grace. Following the example of the Master, pray concerning our own relationship to God and proceed to pray for our family, for the Church, and for the world.

In our age, where so many are "searching for meaning," we can easily get caught up in our relationship with God, our petitions, our wants, and our needs that we forget the needs of others. If we want to grow in our prayer life, however, we must keep others in mind as we come to God. We must exercise a true priestly ministry in seeking to bring to the throne of grace those who are in need of prayer.

Religious leaders in all ages – saints such as Polycarp, Augustine of Hippo, Francis of Assisi, Wesley, Luther, Mary Slessor of Calabar, G. Campbell Morgan, and Mother Teresa of our own day – have been deeply conscious of the needs of their fellow human beings, whom they consistently commended in their prayers.

Some in every age feel that they have been called to a special ministry – offering prayers of intercession. One contemporary religious leader has established a worldwide ministry of intercession. Moreover, the world famous evangelist, Billy Graham, tells that one of his daughters spends literally hours on her knees every morning. Why? Because she has a deep conviction that God has called her to the ministry of intercession.

Thus, in offering the prayer of intercession, in participating in this truly priestly method of ministry, we are, indeed, "treading where the saints have trod," and are treading!

Twice Blessed

As we offer the prayer of intercession, our own spiritual life is greatly strengthened and enriched. We develop to the point where we cannot pray without thinking of others! We find that our prayer life is incomplete unless we offer prayer for others. We are not satisfied to receive our blessing in prayer unless, by means of intercession, we become the source of blessing for others. As the heirs of Abraham, our prayer is that we may become a means of great blessing and so grow in our own spiritual strength.

In a sense, intercession is the spiritual expression of one of the greatest virtues that the Master bids us practice – mercy. Shakespeare said, "The quality of mercy is twice blessed. It blesses him that gives and him that takes." So is the quality of the prayer of intercession!

The prayer of intercession is twice blessed! It blesses the one for whom prayer is offered. Even the most hardened of persons, even those who admittedly are not deeply religious, even those who claim to be atheists, are comforted to know that "someone is praying for me." Very seldom does anyone ever refuse the offer of prayers. The prayer of intercession is a deep source of blessing as prayers are offered for the nation, for society, and for those in need.

Intercession not only blesses those for whom prayer is offered. The prayer of intercession also blesses the one who prays!

As we intercede, we are lifted from the bonds of our narrow concerns and interests to consider the needs of others. When we think about our own problems, we imagine that they are the greatest in the world. Our bills may be high and our cash low; we may not enjoy the best of health; we may be tempted to engage in self-pity. As we reflect upon the needs of others, however, we realize that our problems pale in comparison.

At such times, we should offer prayer for those in need. We should "stand in the gap," praying like Abraham for the wicked and wayward, like Moses for those who are backsliding in their faith and ministry, praying like our Lord Himself for the unity of His people here on earth. As we lift our hearts in prayer to God for others, we realize how great is their need and how necessary it is for us to offer prayer for them. We do what we can, by the grace of God, to relieve their condition.

As we pray in this way, we realize that spiritual power is being made available for the benefit of others. It is by nature deeply satisfying. Thus, we arise from offering prayer for others, exhausted and drained, but at the same time deeply satisfied and joyful in the assurance that we have contributed to the well being of another child of God!

Following the example of the Master, let us continually offer prayer for the welfare of the members of our families and our friends, for the edification of our fellow members of the Body of Christ, and, indeed, for all who dwell upon "this celestial ball."

Using our Master at prayer as an example (John 17), let's examine an outline to help us in interceding for others.

Offering Prayers of Intercession

Invocation

Acknowledge the greatness of God (praise). This may also include acknowledging the goodness of God (thanksgiving); acknowledging the graciousness of God (petition); and acknowledging the mercy of God (confession).

Prayers of Intercession

1. The Family. Pray for your immediate family circle, both your family of orientation and your family of procreation. Include your spouse, children, grandchildren, parents, brothers, and sisters. Don't forget your extended family – cousins, uncles, aunts, in-laws, and any other members of your household. Do you have any close friends who are like family to you? Pray for them as well.

2. The Household of Faith. Intercede for sick and "shut in" members of your local congregation. Include prayer for members, officers, and your pastors. Don't forget church leaders and officers – bishops, clergy, deacons, elders, etc. Remember all those laypersons who serve in the church. Pray for the youth ministry and the mission of the church. Don't forget those who are serving abroad.

3. Persons with Special Needs. Intercede for those who are sick and suffering from certain diseases of the body, such as cancer, heart disease, diabetes, and most pertinently at this time, AIDS. Include people suffering from disorders of the mind and couples whose marriages are "on the rocks." Remember persons who work in dangerous occupations and who educate today's youth. Pray for those who are undergoing great stress and anxiety in their lives. You may know people faced with crucial decisions affecting their future – important exams, job interviews, etc.

4. Our Community and Nation. Pray for those in positions of authority – the head of state, ministers of government, civil servants, judges, and those who uphold the law. Ask God to work through those in the helping professions – doctors, nurses, hospital workers. Ask for wisdom for those in the field of education. May God give strength to youth leaders and people who give their time and energy in serving the needy in our community. Allow your prayers to encourage those who are engaged in community service, especially those who serve on a voluntary basis. Finally, pray for those who are especially concerned for the preservation of the earth's treasures, the creation of our God.

5. *The World.* Intercede for the leaders of the nations of the world, including the office of the United Nations. Pray for those who are engaged in efforts to bring about peace and justice in the world. Pray that those who are in positions of authority would exert a godly influence. Don't forget the many who suffer persecution because of their faith. Include the ecumenical movement and those who are engaged in dialogue with believers of other faiths. Intercede for those engaged in rescue work at the international level and those engaged in steps to bring about reconciliation between warring parties/nations. May those engaged in the fight for justice bring godly intervention for the downtrodden.

6. *Our Enemies.* Jesus told us to "pray for those who despitefully use you." Let us bring before the throne of grace any person whom we regard as an enemy, those who have been hostile, unforgiving, or unkind to us. Pray for your enemies and they may become your friends.

7. *Prayers for the Conversion of Sinners.* A special time of prayer should be reserved for those who are in need of salvation. We should be constantly offering prayers of intercession that more people may turn from their sins and find the grace of God.

A Prayer for Reconciliation

Today there are great pressures upon the institution of marriage. Many countries have a high divorce rate. Many couples experience major difficulties in keeping their marriages fresh, pure, and meaningful over a long period. Often, they turn to the Church for help. As such, an important ministry of the Church is counseling, which includes prayer for the healing of broken relationships.

This prayer can be used especially for those who are facing such difficulties yet desire their marriage to be successful and happy.

O Lord, Behold this couple whose marriage is "on the rocks." Once they were happy together, but today they are not happy. Once they lived in peace and harmony, but now their relationship is marred by disharmony. Once they did things together, but today they do everything separately. Once they admired and cared for each other. Now they do not care for each other. Once they had a sparkle and glow in their relationship, but now it has gone sour and they quarrel all the time.

Yet, O Lord, they want the marriage to work. Heal their marriage! Help them to love each other again. Restore to them that deep, pure love of their early days together. You Who blessed the marriage feast at Cana, sanctify this marriage with Thy presence. O Thou Who hast taught us that "Love fulfills the law" and "Who, for the love of mankind, did send Your divine Son into the world," enable this estranged couple to love each other again that they may continue in Your divine love until their lives end.

Bless them and keep them together in the bonds of matrimonial love through Jesus Christ we pray. Amen.

May these guidelines provide a springboard to launch you into the spiritual depths that await those who pray for the needs of others.

Chapter 7

Prayer is Listening

Does God answer prayer? Will God answer my prayer? Does God, the Creator of the whole universe, care for me? Will you pray for me?

Each day we receive questions just like these. People really want to know whether their prayers are answered. Burdened by their concerns, worries, and problems, they wonder whether God really cares for them. Indeed, throughout the ages, questions on the nature of prayer have been asked of Christians.

We live in times when the whole matter of prayer is being contested. Some wonder whether God can really make a difference in the affairs of mankind. Many believe God created the universe, leaving mankind to "run its affairs." In this age of high technology and human achievement, the question of the nature of prayer is most urgent. We must ask, in all sincerity, "Does God answer prayer?"

When I was a child, I used to visit an elderly aunt. A very devout Christian, she had a number of Christian plaques and decorations in the house. One read: "Every prayer is answered in God's way."

Over the years, those words never left me. I do not recall who wrote them or where she obtained this poster. All I know is that its message is very real. It clearly affirmed that God does answer prayer.

This is certainly in keeping with what the Bible teaches about God. One truth is clear: God is a personal God whose ears are open to the cries of mankind.

When Abraham prayed to God for the wicked cities of Sodom and Gomorrah, the Lord responded. Although these cities were eventually destroyed because they lacked ten righteous men, it is clear that God was willing to give Abraham a hearing (Genesis 18:18-33). The Lord also heard the cry of the Israelites when they suffered in bondage in Egypt, and He delivered them through the marvelous ministry of Moses His servant (Exodus 3:1-12; 14:1-31; 15:1-21). Moreover, Moses approached God on several occasions, deeply convinced that He was a God Whose ears were open to the cries of His people.

The great prophet Elijah, in his encounter with the prophets of Baal on Mount Carmel, prayed to God and believed that He would answer in a dramatic display of His power. Jesus, in the Prayer of the Great High Priest, offered intercession for Christians in all ages (John 17).

These biblical examples show that God is a personal God Who hears the cries of mankind. Idols made from wood and stone, however, "have mouths that cannot speak, and eyes that cannot see; they have ears that cannot hear" (Psalm 115:5,6, NEB). God's ears are ever open to the cries of mankind.

The God revealed in Christ as divine love answers the prayers of those who come to Him in sincerity. But how does God answer prayer? Is it always in the affirmative? Does He sometimes simply tell us "no"? How might we expect God to respond to our prayers?

When God Answers "Yes"

There are blessed times when God hears our prayer and responds with a clear, unequivocal "yes". For example, Hannah earnestly prayed to God for a son, and her petition was granted. The Bible says, "The Lord remembered her" (1 Samuel 1:19). When God "remembers" someone, it is a sign of divine blessing, of granting a special request, or helping an individual in a very special way. The Bible teaches that God does answer prayer!

People undoubtedly ask, "Does He answer prayer today?" This is a burning issue for contemporary man. Because God doesn't change, He still answers prayer today.

Our God is a good and wonderful God. Can He still work miracles? Listen to the testimony of Mrs. Onis Sinclair, a young lady whose son was born with a defective heart. Her story shows us what kind of God we serve.

Our ordeal started on March 8, 1978, when a baby boy of six pounds, five ounces was born to my husband and me at the Princess Margaret Hospital in Nassau.

From day one the baby was like a crying cymbal. He was baptized at the Ebenezer Manse where the minister, the Rev. Patterson Deane, remarked that "boys will be boys" when the baby cried persistently. I knew differently, however.

No one was aware of his illness, but his constant cries gave everyone great concern. He was bluish in color, and his feet were so swollen that it felt like you could pick his toes off.

During his four-week check-up, the examining doctor startled me. When she listened to his heart, she jumped back in amazement. "Is anything wrong?" I asked. Trying not to sound alarmed, she gently responded, "Go to the front desk and ask the nurse to make an appointment to see Dr. Maud Stevenson at her clinic at the Princess Margaret Hospital on Friday of this week." Not knowing what to expect, I could not wait to get to the clinic. The baby continued his cries and sleepless days and nights as I waited for Friday to come.

We arrived at the clinic only to find out that it was the Heart Clinic where children with heart disorders are brought. I was scared. Dr. Stevenson was beautiful. She was also gentle, kind, and reassuring.

After examining Hansen, she told me that he had a heart problem, but it could be corrected. I got his medication and left the hospital.

My job now was to break the news to my husband when he returned to Nassau. I knew whatever I told him would not make a difference in his attitude toward me and the child. When I caught him in a good mood, I told him what the doctor had said. He accepted the explanation without reservation.

My main task had now begun. For the first year of his life, Hansen lived in and out of the hospital. He never stayed at home for more than four weeks at a time. I lost my job after he was born, but I accepted it as part of God's plan. He knew that I could not go to work with the problems Hansen faced.

On April 3, 1979, Hansen was admitted to Jackson Memorial Hospital for tests and possible surgery. His first surgery was done the following day. Doctors used a portion of his liver to patch a hole in the aorta. Five days later he returned to Nassau as a more relaxed baby who would now sleep at nights and take his food.

In August of that year, he took his first baby step. I rejoiced as I knew God was with me and that there was hope. I prayed night and day for God to help me to handle the situation in the best way possible. He did. I returned to work that same summer.

Hansen made good progress after the first operation. His hospital visits decreased from weekly to monthly, to quarterly to half yearly. He entered school at age six. I informed his teacher of his condition and asked her to look for symptoms such as bluish discoloration, shortness of breath, drowsiness, nausea, and fainting. Should he experience any of these warning signs, she should call me right away. The child would need to be taken to the hospital immediately. She understood and promised to notify me of any changes.

On September 24, 1984, the day the eye of hurricane David was over Nassau, I had to take Hansen to Jackson Memorial Hospital because he was experiencing great difficulty in almost all the areas mentioned above. He was admitted to the hospital that night, so I returned to Nassau the following day only to find out that my father had passed away the day before, the same day I took Hansen to Jackson Memorial Hospital. Without losing any time, I grabbed Donna and Onissa and prepared to leave Nassau for Jamaica the following day. My husband was at sea.

My father was buried October 4, 1984. Hansen's second surgery on October 6 corrected his auricles. He returned to Nassau on October 16 and continued at school as usual.

Since the second operation, his hospital visits remained at twice yearly and his health has greatly improved. The doctors advised me that he needed a third and final surgery, but they were being cautious as they anticipated an all-day procedure. They said that he had combined every possible heart disorder that anyone could think of and more!

In August of 1988, the doctors finally agreed to perform surgery again. Hansen was admitted to Jackson Memorial Hospital on September 4 for surgery on September 8. Can God still work miracles? Yes, He can!

Hundreds of prayers were offered on Hansen's behalf, before and during surgery. Instead of an all-day, tiring surgery, the procedure was completed in two and a half hours! Miraculous, isn't it? My God is able. From Hansen's illness, I've come to trust Him more each day.

For the first time in his life, Hansen was able to walk without fainting or tiring. He did not win a trophy at Omnifest '88, but he is a winner as he successfully completed the mile on January 28, 1989.

I believe God chose me to look after this boy, soon to be 11 years old. During his illness, I was never downcast. I tried my best to encour-

age him. From the day I discovered Hansen's illness, I knew I had to be strong, devoted, patient, caring, and understanding to his cause. From the doctor's first report on Hansen's condition, I knew I had to trust God for sustenance and guidance during this ordeal.

My thanks to all of you who prayed with me and for me, and a special thank you to God for choosing me to mother this boy. Thanks also go to the Sassoon Heart Association, who stood by me all the way.[1]

Her testimony proves that "with God, nothing shall be impossible" (Luke 1:37). His true greatness can be reflected in your life and through any circumstance.

Perhaps God has chosen you to tackle a difficult task just to test your faith. Hold on and allow God to have His way. Yes, God does answer prayer. He is a miracle-working God. His ears are still open to the cries of all who call upon Him in sincerity. This is precisely why we can approach His throne boldly with our petitions. Since we are coming to the King of kings and the Lord of lords, we can bring big and bold petitions with us to the throne of grace.

When God Says "No"

Because He is a powerful God and Sovereign Lord over the universe, He does not always answer in the affirmative. Sometimes God may tell us "no".

Take Moses, for example. In the final days of his earthly sojourn, he led the Israelites to the border of the Promised Land. Standing at the banks of the Jordan River, the great patriarch had one burning desire — to enter the Promised Land. He wanted nothing more than to cross the Jordan and spend his last days in the land of milk and honey. But God denied this request.

Just think of it! Moses had led the children of Israel out of Egypt, their place of bondage. By the grace of God, Moses had performed miracles before them in the wilderness. Moses had been the divinely appointed mediator of the covenant and the Law (Exodus 19,20).

Scripture tells us that Moses was so close to God that he spoke to God "as a man speaketh unto his friend" (Exodus 33:11). When this godly man prayed earnestly that he might cross the Jordan, God rejected his request. How did God answer Moses? "Let it suffice thee; speak no more unto me of this matter" (Deuteronomy 3:26).

In other words, God told Moses, "You have done your part. Be content with what I've given you to do." God directed him to charge Joshua with this task. God's response was clear — Moses was not to cross the Jordan; he would, however, designate another to do so. The great patriarch left this life with his fondest desire denied!

Sometimes God says no to us. We may desire certain things with a great passion. God may intervene, however, and change our plans.

Dr. Thomas Coke was the great pioneer of the missionary endeavors of Methodism. Short in stature, like the biblical Zaccheus, he was nevertheless a dynamo who always sought to proclaim the Gospel in faraway places. He accomplished a tremendous amount of missionary work, covering an amazing amount of territory by land and sea — before the jet age!

He, along with Asbury, was instrumental in establishing Methodism in America in 1784. Christmas day 1786 found him in Antigua, kindling the flame of Methodism already lit by that illustrious layman Nathaniel Gilbert. In 1789 he was in Jamaica, where he also established Methodism.

Coke, however, had a consuming desire to spread the message of Methodism, the saving grace of God in Christ, to the peoples of the Far East. Desiring to serve in India and Ceylon, he set sail for the Far East. He never made it. He died and was buried at sea. Coke had finished his task. When he went further afield, God intervened and stopped him.[2]

God does say no in various ways. The great Scots New Testament scholar William Barclay, in one of his commentaries, made this solemn statement: "We would save ourselves a lot of worry if we realized that certain things were not for us." This is so true. If we can recognize when God is saying "no" to us, and govern our lives accordingly, we would spare ourselves from many unnecessary concerns — and ulcers! May we pray:

God grant me the courage to change the things I can.
The grace to accept the things I cannot.
And the wisdom to know the difference.[3]

When God Says to Wait

Sometimes God answers "yes". Sometimes He says "no". Often the answer to our prayer is not immediately clear. In such situations, we can conclude that God wants us to wait.

When Lazarus' sisters sent an urgent message to Jesus, asking Him to come immediately because their brother was ill, the Lord did not rush to the scene. He waited for a few days in a village before leaving for Bethany. By the time He arrived, Lazarus was dead and buried.

Martha, the action-oriented sister of the dead disciple, met Jesus and rebuked Him for tarrying so long. With remorse and sorrow, she rasped, "If you had been here, sir, my brother would not have died" (John 11:21, NEB). Martha, who was always anxious to act, could not understand why Jesus did respond immediately when they had called Him.

Jesus had a reason for His delay. When the distressed sisters first summoned Jesus, His words implied a higher purpose: "This illness will not end in death; it has come for the glory of God, to bring glory to the Son of God" (John 11:4, NEB).

That's when Jesus performed the greatest of His miracles, or as John prefers to call them, "signs" — the raising of Lazarus from the dead. He proclaimed the great hope that is at the heart of the Gospel: "I am the resurrection, and the life: he that believeth in me, though he were dead, yet shall he live" (John 11:25). These words have brought comfort to countless millions over the centuries who have faced death.

Martha and Mary, the sisters of Lazarus, had to learn that God does not always work according to human timetables. They were anxious for Him to come to the rescue of their sick brother. He came in His time and accomplished more than they could ever expect. In raising Lazarus from the dead, He demonstrated that the Gospel speaks of a power that conquers even death and brings hope to the bereaved.

The Bible, in its many messages about prayer, often teaches us to wait. Because we live in a high-speed age, our generation has to learn this lesson repeatedly. We constantly try to find shortcuts and produce instant results. We find it hard to be patient. Yet, if we are to develop our prayer life, we must learn to wait.

Waiting is not mere resignation but an expectant tarrying. Its watchful attitude humbly and confidently waits upon God. It is by no means resignation but *expectation with confidence.*

Moses exhorted the Israelites at the Red Sea to wait and see what the Lord would do for them. Moses knew that God would intervene to assist the Israelites. They only had to wait for His instructions.

The Gospel of Luke tells us about a couple who were waiting. Zacharias and Elizabeth, the pious parents of John, anticipated the coming of the Messiah. The answer to God is not always immediate. Let us learn this. Often God's answer is wait. The psalmist sums it up well: "Wait on the Lord: be of good courage, and he shall strengthen thine heart: wait, I say, on the Lord" (Psalm 27:14).

When God Wants You to Grow

Sometimes God's answer is very clear, and He gives us a yes or no. Sometimes He advises us to be patient and wait. There are also times when He intends to teach us an important lesson for our spiritual development. In these situations, God tells us to grow.

The apostle Paul had an experience that differed greatly from that of Moses or Hannah. He suffered from an illness that caused him great physical pain. This malady was so hurtful that he called it a "messenger of Satan" (2 Cor. 12:7). While some scholars have suggested his malady might have been an eye disease or malaria, we really do not know what plagued Paul. We do know, however, that it caused him a great deal of suffering. On three occasions, the apostle earnestly asked God to remove this affliction, but Paul was not healed of this disease. Does that mean God had not answered his prayer? By no means.

God's answer can be found in these profound words: "My grace is sufficient for thee: for my strength is made perfect in weakness" (2 Cor. 12:9).

No, God did not heal Paul's disease. God did assure the apostle that His grace was sufficient to keep him. God was with him and teaching him. Through this experience the apostle Paul improved his own spiritual life. He realized that in our own human illness we often learn to depend on the strength and power of God.

God may not answer your prayer in the way that you expect. He may speak to you, however, so that your spiritual life may be deepened. Nothing satisfies the soul like sincere, heartfelt prayer. As we pray, we develop spiritually and by the grace of God come to the measure of the fullness of the stature of Christ.

Let us remember always that the Christian life is a process of growth. As we come to Christ, we are led to a deeper understanding of the meaning of Christian suffering and Christian fortitude. Prayer enables us to grow spiritually and to graduate from being fed milk as babes to eating the meat of the Word as mature believers.

The Meaning of Prayer

When we appreciate the fact that God's answer to our prayer comes in terms of our spiritual growth, we begin to understand the true meaning of prayer. Our popular concept of prayer is in terms of expressing our wants and needs to God. Petition is certainly an important aspect of prayer. Simply put, prayer is asking God for things.

But is this the essence of prayer? Doesn't prayer have more to do with seeking the will of God than asking Him for things? The example of our Lord in the Garden of Gethsemane can teach us important truths.

On the night of His betrayal, Jesus went to the Garden of Gethsemane. His enemies were pursuing Him. He was deeply conscious that the Cross of Calvary cast its shadow over the closing days of His earthly ministry. Yet, being truly human and divine, He knew the heavy burden of the Cross.

Jesus then came with his disciples to a place called Gethsemane. He said to them, "Sit here while I go over there to pray." He took with him Peter and the two sons of Zebedee. Anguish and dismay came over him, and he said to them, "My heart is ready to break with grief. Stop here, and stay awake with me." He went on a little, fell on His face in prayer, and said, "My Father, if it is possible, let this cup pass me by. Yet, not as I will, but as thou wilt" (Matthew 26:26-39, NEB).

As we meditate upon this profoundly moving passage, we are deeply aware of the humanity of Jesus. As one with mankind, He knew the pains and deep emotional weaknesses of human flesh. And so He expressed His own wish — that the cup of suffering of Calvary should pass. But at the same time He placed a higher priority upon the divine will. That's why He could say at the end of this session of deep communion with His Heavenly Father, "My Father, if it is not possible for this cup to pass me by without my drinking it, thy will be done" (Matthew 26:42, NEB).

"Thy will be done." Isn't it precisely in this expression, which calls for obedience to God's will, that we find the key to the meaning of prayer? Understood in its most profound significance, prayer essentially seeks to know the will of God rather than seeks to bend the will of God to our own. In prayer, then, we seek not so much to ask God to do things for us as to seek what may be His will for us!

"Thy will be done." Significantly, this expression is found not only in the model prayer the Lord gave to His disciples but also in this intimate time of communion with His Heavenly Father before His suffering and death.

"Thy will be done." In prayer we repeatedly ask God for things that we would like. Often we make our plans and just ask God to sanction what we have already decided. This is "putting the cart before the horse." First, we should approach God and seek His will. Then we can serve Him with confidence. Only as we know God's will can we seek His strength to do what is pleasing in His sight.

Yes, the motto I saw in my aunt's living room is true:

"Every prayer is answered in God's way."

God does answer us in various ways. When we come to Him in prayer, He often answers us "yes". As Sovereign Lord of the universe, His answer may sometimes be "no". As the One Who is in ultimate control of the affairs of mankind, there are times when God wants us to wait. He bids us to be patient and not to force the pace of events. Many times, however, our Loving Father wants us to grow. He teaches us, on the anvil of experience, to grow spiritually even as we seek His will. He assures us, "My grace is sufficient for thee: for my strength is made perfect in weakness" (2 Cor. 12:9).

Let us come to the throne of grace, confident that God does answer prayer. Let us be persistent in prayer. Let us be trusting in prayer. Let us be faithful in prayer. Most of all, let us ever seek to know His will for our lives. Once we know His will, may we have the strength to do the same.

Are You Listening?

Since every prayer is answered in God's way, then the question naturally comes to mind, "How does one receive God's answer?" The answer is to listen.

This writer remembers a well-known Baptist minister preaching a sermon on prayer in a small church in the Jamaican countryside. Comparing prayer to a telephone conversation, he pointed out that it involves both speaking and listening.

"When we ask the other party a question, we don't just hang up the phone!" Looking around at the small congregation, he paused and then delivered his statement on prayer: "We wait! We wait for an answer!"[4]

The minister emphasized that in prayer we should also wait for God's answer. He advised the members of his congregation to pause for a few moments at the end of their prayer and to listen for what God has to say to them. The same point was more recently made by a young Methodist minister preaching to a much larger congregation gathered in worship in Nassau, Bahamas.[5]

Surely, these ministers of the Gospel stress an important lesson for us to keep in mind as we pursue our prayer life. How many of us regard our prayer as a telephone conversation, one in which we approach God with our own concerns and petitions and in which we wait to hear God's response to us?

Yes, prayer is offering praise and thanks to God. Prayer is asking God for things. Prayer involves bringing others before the throne of grace. These facets comprise only one side of prayer — the human approach to God.

But what of the other, which is just as important — the divine response? If we are to grow at all in our prayer life, then we must wait to hear what God has in store for us.

Listening is essential for our spiritual growth in prayer! We must be prepared to listen, to be sensitive to God's word to us. The old man Eli, when approached by Samuel in the temple, advised the boy to listen to the Lord and to say, "Speak, Lord; for thy servant heareth" (1 Samuel 3:9).

This must be our stance in prayer. Having offered our prayers to God, having made known to Him our requests and having sought blessings for others, it is only right that we should wait upon the Lord. This waiting is both active and passive. It means that we are sensitive to the prompting of the Spirit. Thus, we may learn whether God's answer is positive — yes; negative — no; deliberative — wait; or instructive — grow!

Let us be good listeners. Our prayer life cannot be effective if we are not prepared to listen to God's voice speaking to us and directing us in the way we ought to go. Like Samuel in the temple, we must listen to what God has to say to us and act in accord with His answer.

What should be our attitude after we have given our praises to God, thanked Him for His blessings, made our petitions, confessed our sins, and laid our concerns for others before the throne of grace? We need to say, "I am listening for You, Lord. What do You have to say to me?"

Yes, prayer is listening. Our spiritual ears may be dull of hearing, however, and we need to cultivate this spiritual sense. It is important that we do not give up in learning to discern God's voice.

Message from the Wayside Pulpit

The Wayside Pulpit at Trinity Church, Frederick Street, is one of the most arresting sights in Nassau. Each day thousands of Bahamians and tourists alike pass the busy intersection where the church is located. There on a corner is The Wayside Pulpit, prominently displayed, giving its sage advice to everyone who passes by. Day in and day out, it preaches a message with a Christian theme.

On several occasions the message came to me with particular relevance. Early in 1988, for instance, I read the message, which consisted of four simple words: Continue steadfastly in prayer.

So often in prayer we are inclined to give up. This is especially the case when we face the problem of unanswered prayer. Many people indeed have told of how they became discouraged and failed to remain steadfast in prayer.

Yet, if our prayer life is to be developed, we must be persistent. It is not enough to just pray "when we feel like it." Nor should we resort to prayer only when we are in trouble. During these times, we are especially close to God and are more than ever in need of prayer.

But prayer requires that we be consistent! We should continue to pray not only when we are in need but when we are in good health, when everything seems to be going our way and all is well. In all our trials and tribulations, as well as our joys and triumphs, we must turn to the Lord in prayer that He, by His grace, may deliver us and keep us from going the wrong way. As we continue our journey through life, let us constantly turn to Him in prayer.

We sometimes use the expression "prayer warriors" for those who pray earnestly like the prophet Elijah. They are the people who continue steadfastly in prayer and are constantly on the move. Let us remember them also in their moments of prayer to the Lord. It is only as we continue steadfastly in prayer that we shall be enabled to win the victory.

Chapter 8

Prayer is Work

Someone once said, "Whenever I am in trouble I pray. And since I'm always in trouble, there is not a day when I don't pray." There are no shortcuts to spiritual growth, and prayer is the path we must walk. Prayer, however, is also hard work.

We live in an age of rapid communication and travel. Jet-propelled aircraft, moving at supersonic speeds, whisk passengers to their destinations in hours. Formerly, such trips took days, even weeks. Space vehicles, moving at even higher speeds, bolt through the atmosphere, lifting interplanetary travel from the realm of science fiction to that of distinct possibility. Telephones and fax messages, working at very high speeds, take only seconds to transmit auditory and visual messages over thousands of miles. With technological advances in computers, an entire industry finds it necessary to measure their operations in minute fractions of a second.

All this has brought about a great demand for things to be done in a hurry. We live for instant results, which explains the rapid growth in "fast food" establishments and products that can be processed rapidly.

While our obsession with speed may be useful in technological fields, it is not desirable in our spiritual life. This is especially true regarding prayer. Yes, it takes only a few moments for us to offer prayer to God wherever we may be. But the development of our prayer life is not something that can be accomplished instantly. It requires much effort over a very long period. It is precisely for this reason that the most devout saints throughout the ages testify that the cultivation of one's prayer life is a lifetime process.

As we have noted already, the disciples asked Jesus, "Lord, teach us to pray." They recognized prayer to be an essential component of a person's spiritual development, requiring constant effort and nurture. Prayer may be truly described as a discipline. As such, *prayer can be learned.*

This learning process must be carried out over a long period in a very disciplined manner. Hurry is to be avoided in the cultivation of one's prayer life. Today, in our age of speed, we must heed the warning of the saints. *Hurry is the death of devotion.*

We must develop our prayer life because it is at the heart of our spiritual well being! For that reason, we need to be intentional and determined in the cultivation of our prayer life.

"A Time for Everything"

"For everything there is a time . . ." So writes the sage who gave us the Book of Ecclesiastes. Knowing the proper time for things is crucial. In many situations, timing is the major factor that determines the success or failure of a given action.

We must set apart definite times for the practice of prayer. Although we are free to offer prayer wherever it's convenient for us, three particular times seem especially conducive to our prayer life: early morning, noon, and night.

The psalmist puts it aptly: "Evening, and morning, and at noon, will I pray, and cry aloud: and he shall hear my voice" (Psalm 55:17).

First, we should begin the day with prayer. The Bible shows us that the great spiritual and administrative leaders began the day with prayer. Abraham, Moses, and Elijah rose up early in the morning to pray. It is recorded of the Master Himself: "Very early the next morning, long before daylight, Jesus got up and left the house. He went out of town to a lonely place, where he prayed" (Mark 1:35, GNB).

This tradition of praying early in the morning has continued throughout the ages. The Church Fathers, in their writings, testify that they found the early morning particularly useful for prayer. Martin Luther spent hours each day in prayer, beginning early in the morning. John Wesley arose at 4:00 a.m. each day to pray. Indeed, the secret of the spiritual power of these giants of the Christian faith was their prayer life, which began early in the morning. This practice continues today.

I recall a young man telling me about his mother. Every morning, as soon as she opened her eyes, she turned to God in prayer. "Before she did anything, even before she put on her slippers, she prayed," he testified.

There can be no better way to begin the day than in prayer! Indeed, early in the morning, while the day is still fresh, while the rising sun shines upon the grass, while our minds are still uncluttered by the concerns of the day, it is good to pray to the God of creation. Early in the morning, as we reflect upon the day before us, we can pray for divine guidance in all our undertakings.

Two elements tend to dominate our morning devotion: praise and petition. Begin the day by offering praise to God as our Creator. Reflect upon His Majesty and allow the words to flow from the depths of your soul.

We also make our petitions to God in the morning. As we think about the day ahead, we may pray for wisdom and strength to meet its challenges. This is why the morning devotional period has been referred to as offering "strength for the day." In our morning prayer we seek spiritual strength to carry us through the day. Yes, it is the best time to offer praise and present our petitions to God.

Mid-day prayer is often forgotten. Many of us are very busy with our various jobs in the office, classroom, store, or workroom. We may not have a lot of time for prayer. Still, in the midst of these activities, we can pause to whisper a short prayer, seeking divine blessings and guidance as we carry out our responsibilities.

There is a growing trend in some offices for workers to get together and pray during their lunch break. Such office prayer meetings undoubtedly provide a major means of spiritual renewal in our community. Keep in mind, however, that we should never allow our spiritual exercises to interfere with the proper performance of our duties on the job.

Mary Slessor, the famous Scots missionary who served for many years in West Africa, had no patience with the students in her Christian boarding school who had their prayer time whenever there were dishes to be washed!

Our mid-day or morning prayers at the office should not, in any way, impede us in our work. Rather, such prayer should make us more pleasant and efficient workers! Yes, prayer and work should go together.

The Church has always regarded the evening as a special time for prayer. In the Middle Ages, for instance, when the Monastic movement was influential and extensive, the monks engaged in well-prepared corporate prayer in the evening. The evening devotional time was known as "Compline."

Young people who participate in Christian camps in the outdoors often find evening prayers, around a campfire, very inspiring.

Two major elements comprise evening prayer. First, there is *thanksgiving*, which, as has been seen, is very close to *praise*. As we think about the activities of the day, we can do nothing but thank God for His many blessings so bountifully provided for us. Yes, the evening is a time for thanksgiving!

The other element of evening prayer is *confession*. As we reflect upon the day's activities, we may remember moments when we failed the Master by being unkind or dishonest. We may have committed acts that were not worthy of those who profess to follow Christ. As these incidents come to mind, we must turn to God and ask for His pardon and cleansing. A very beautiful evening prayer says words to this effect:

And since being human, we could not have passed this day without sinning against Thy Divine Majesty in some way, we pray for Thy forgiveness.

How beautiful and relevant those words are to us. Our sinful, selfish world is in need of the forgiving love of God. We come to the end of the day, thanking God for His goodness and praying for His forgiveness for the sins we have committed. Having confessed our failings and shortcomings, we listen to God. Ransomed, healed, and forgiven, we can doze off into a restful and refreshing sleep with our conscience clear. No riches compare to being at peace with God, others, and ourselves!

A Chapel in Your Home

Just as we should have definite times set apart for prayer, we should have specific places reserved for prayer. Because peace and quiet are essential to nurturing our prayer life, we need a quiet place where we can be alone with God.

Noise surrounds us. Our homes are often crowded, making it difficult to be alone. With a little imagination and ingenuity, however, you can find a place in most homes where you can be alone with God. Having a place for prayer will help you to cultivate your spiritual life.

It is not enough for us to be solitary in our prayer life. In the context of the home, we should participate in family devotions. We must have a special place set apart in the home for family devotions. ("Set apart" indicates a "holy place," one dedicated to the worship of God.) In my own case, this place inevitably turned out to be the master bedroom just before bedtime. Indeed, our children have fallen asleep when my wife and I prayed too long!

Having a place for prayer in the home is ideal, but sometimes it's just not convenient. You may have overcrowding, unexpected responsibilities, etc. If you want to improve your prayer life, you can find a place in the garden. You may want to go for a morning or evening walk in the neighborhood. Many have found themselves deeply inspired especially during walks when they relish the wonders of God's creation.

You may have a particular place that brings back memories of some deep spiritual experience. One minister tells of how he returned to such a place whenever he was in need of spiritual rejuvenation. For most of us, however, we must find within the home a place to cultivate our souls.

At one time, very large homes often had a built-in chapel. This is hardly ever the case today. When new homeowners give you a tour, they proudly point to their living room, dining room, bedroom, kitchen, etc. Some homes even have a built-in bar. Think of it. Where large homes once had a chapel, now some large homes have a bar.

This reveals the spiritual condition of our generation. We need to get rid of the bar and install a chapel in our homes. We don't need to build a large home to have a chapel. Every home, no matter how small or humble, can have a place where we can meet God as individuals, families, or a community group for prayer. Some may be able to build a chapel in their homes, but we can all set aside a place for prayer. Whether your home is small or large, you can reserve a place where you can enter into the holy of holies.

There is a place of quiet rest,
Near to the heart of God.
A place where sin cannot molest,
Near to the heart of God.

You need a "chapel in your home," a place where you and your family can continually draw near to the heart of God.

Improving Your Prayer Life

How, then, should we go about this process of improving our prayer life?

We can begin by carefully evaluating it. Dr. Sangster reminds us that just as we periodically go to our physician for a physical "check up," we should occasionally undergo a spiritual "check up." We need to ask ourselves hard questions about our own devotional life. Here are some questions that we should ponder carefully.

- How much time am I spending in prayer?
- Am I spending enough time in prayer?
- Can I afford to spend more time in prayer than I'm doing now?
- Do I offer praise to God as frequently as I should?
- Considering the blessings that I have received, do I express thanksgiving to God as I should?
- Am I helping other members of my family in their prayer life?
- Am I honest in offering confession?
- Who are some of the people I should be praying for continually?
- Do I know persons who are in special need of prayer?
- Who am I not praying for as I should?
- Are there situations in my home, church, nation, and world about which I should be praying?
- Can I do more to develop my prayer life?
- Is the Lord pleased with my spiritual development?

As you honestly answer these questions, you can begin to improve the areas in which you are weak. If the element of praise is lacking, then you give more time to worshiping God. Use this same method to improve the elements of thanksgiving, petition, and confession in your devotional life.

A Plan for Prayer

If we are to develop a disciplined prayer life, we must pray methodically. We need to develop a plan to help us consistently offer prayer.

This means that we must not be led simply by our emotions. Yes, there will be times when, because of the challenges that we face, our prayer will be more intense and frequent than usual. We should not just pray when "we feel like it" and neglect our prayer life when we're not so inclined.

How can we prevent the inertia that may set in by depending upon our emotions? We should devise a plan or a timetable of some sort to remind ourselves of our responsibility to cultivate our devotional life. Such a plan should not be inflexible; it should merely be a guide to assist us as we seek to be disciplined in the way we approach Our Maker. Why is this so necessary? In prayer, as in so many other avenues of endeavors, *practice makes perfect.*

How can you increase your intercession? Compile a prayer list to strengthen this aspect of prayer. Intercession always adds variety and freshness to our prayer life because there is always so much for us to pray about! We should think about everyone we know who is in special need of prayer. List them, either alphabetically or by their need.

Is there any member of our family who is in need? Do we know of anyone in our church or community who is ill? What about that young person preparing for an important examination? What about that lonely old lady who lives down the street? We should include all such persons in our prayer list.

Think about those who belong to our church. We can also pray for those in authority in our state, nation, and the world. We should think about fellow employees at the office, in the factory, in the store, or in the field. Are any of them in need of prayer?

What prominent problems plague our corner of the world? All these persons and concerns should be included in our prayer list. We might soon discover that our prayer list is much longer than we had expected it to be when we began!

Having completed our prayer list, we should draw up a timetable. Since we cannot include all the needs and concerns in any one prayer session, a timetable helps us to cover all the needs in a specified time, such as a week.

Remember, three periods during the day are especially conducive to developing our prayer life: early morning, noon, and the evening. Take into account these three major periods and seek to include, in the course of a week, all the major concerns that are on our hearts as we draw near to God in prayer.

We must realize that such a prayer timetable is a guide. It can be adapted so that if there are any special concerns, we can give them proper emphasis in our prayer. In the same way, we must consider that the needs and concerns vary from time to time. We should revise our prayer timetable periodically so that we may include new concerns that arise.

Our prayer timetable should be changed at least once every three months. We may find it necessary to do so much more frequently. If need be, we should not hesitate to do so. Our prayer life should not be allowed to become routine, perfunctory, and stale. Our times of prayer should be new every morning as we grow in the grace and knowledge of God and in our concern for the welfare of others.

You may consider this suggested timetable as a model for your own prayer time:

My Prayer Timetable

"Lord, teach us to pray, as John also taught his disciples" (Luke 11:1).

DAY	MORNING	NOON	EVENING/NIGHT
Sunday			
Monday			
Tuseday			
Wednesday			
Thursday			
Friday			
Saturday			

The above list can be used as a basis for drawing up a weekly prayer timetable. In the morning the emphasis may be on adoration, thanksgiving, and petition. In the evening, the emphasis may be on thanksgiving and confession. Prayers of intercession should be included in all prayer times.

Time allotted to prayer will vary according to the temperament, needs, and conditions under which we live. Generally speaking, about 15-20 minutes should be given to morning prayer; 5-10 minutes may be devoted to prayer at noon; and 15-20 minutes should be allocated to evening prayer. Whatever time we devote to prayer, however, the attitude of our hearts should be marked by sincerity and compassion.

Prayer of Adoration

A prayer of adoration to God the Father, Son, and Holy Spirit can consist of innovations based on Scripture (especially the Psalms), the verses of a hymn, etc.

Prayer of Thanksgiving

Reflect upon the things that we can thank God for — the gift of a new day, life, health, strength, our family and friends, our nation, salvation, etc.

Prayer of Petition

Ask God to help us in our own specific situations. Here we reflect on our needs for health, prosperity, spiritual growth, etc.

Prayer of Confession

We bring before God our faults and failings, our sins, unwitting and deliberate, and seek divine forgiveness.

For we have not a high priest who is unable to sympathize with our weaknesses, but one who in every respect has been tempted as we are, yet without sinning. Let us then with confidence draw near to the throne of grace, that we may receive mercy and find grace to help in time of need (Hebrews 4:15,16, RSV).

Prayer of Intercession

We bring before the throne of grace our concerns for the needs of others. As mentioned in chapter 6, these may include:

1. Prayers for the members of our family.
2. Prayers for the Church.
3. Prayers for those with special needs.
4. Prayers for our community and nation.
5. Prayers for the world.
6. Prayers for our enemies.
7. Prayers for the conversion of sinners.

Resources for Improving Your Prayer Life

Since the cultivation of our prayer life is a life long process, we must use all the resources that are available to us. We cannot get very far on our own. Our prayers become repetitive, dull, and eventually sterile if we do not make use of these great spiritual resources of the Church, all of which are readily available to us if only we would use them!

First and foremost, the most important resource for developing our prayer life is the Bible. Indeed, Bible study along with prayer are the two main "means of grace" by which our souls are nourished and our spirits revived. Prayer and Bible study are complimentary; to be truthful, no devotional exercise is complete if either of these means of grace is lacking!

The Scriptures enrich our prayer life in many ways. Sometimes as we read the Bible, we are simply led to offer prayer.

Many of the prayers of the Church are based solidly on the Scriptures. Some prayers are really paraphrases of scriptural passages. We can also use the great prayers of the Bible as models to assist in our own prayer life.

Among these we include:

- The prayer of Abraham for the wicked cities (Genesis 18:23-33)
- The prayer offered by Moses for the Israelites
- The prayer of dedication of the temple by Solomon (2 Chronicles 6:14-42)
- The many prayers to be found in the Book of Psalms
- David's great prayer of confession (Psalm 51)
- Turning to the New Testament, we should think of the prayer life of Jesus:
- The prayer of the Great High Priest (Acts 4:23-31)

- The opening verses of some of the apostle Paul's epistles
- The prayers of the Book of Revelation

The Lord's Prayer

Most of all, we should study the model prayer, that unique prayer that Our Lord Himself gave in response to His disciples' request, "Lord, teach us to pray." This is *The Lord's Prayer*, or as some scholars prefer to call it, *The Disciples' Prayer* (Luke 11:2-4; Matthew 6:9-13). Also known as *The Family Prayer*, it is offered by millions of persons countless times every day.

Why is it called a model prayer? These verses contain all the essential elements of prayer:

1. *Praise and adoration:* "Our Father which art in heaven, Hallowed be thy name" (vs. 9).

2. *Petition:* "Thy kingdom come. Thy will be done in earth, as it is in heaven. Give us this day our daily bread.... And lead us not into temptation, but deliver us from evil" (vs. 10-13).

3. *Confession:* "And forgive us our debt" (vs. 12).

4. *Intercession:* "As we forgive our debtors" (vs. 12).

This prayer begins in praise, in acknowledging the Fatherhood of God and in the declaration of His holiness. Prayer, which is praise, should begin here.

We must acknowledge the greatness of God, the Father and Creator of all things. Moreover, the Christian can address God as Father by virtue of the redemptive ministry of Jesus. "How great is the love that the Father has shown to us! We were called God's children, and such we are" (1 John 3:1, NEB).

The invocation continues: "Hallowed be thy name." This may be literally rendered, "May thy name be revered as holy because it is holy." Here we encounter one of the paradoxes of the Christian faith. While we are bid to address God as "Father" in an intimate relationship, we are also to be aware of His holiness, His majesty, and His power.

God alone is holy, and everything else derives its holiness from Him. His name is holy because it belongs to and identifies Him. In this invocation, then, we realize that while we are to draw near to God, and with millions of Christians dare to call Him Father, we must also be aware of His holiness and revere Him as Creator.

There are three petitions in this prayer, and they are quite specific and bold.

First, there is the petition calling for the reign of God to be consummated: "Thy kingdom come. Thy will be done in earth, as it is in heaven" (Matthew 6:10).

The second part of this petition explains the first. The kingdom of God refers to the reign or rule of God over the whole of His creation. The triumph of the kingdom of God means that all live according to the will of God. Christians are to pray fervently for the realization of the reign (rule) of God. In the light of contemporary development in the international political arena, this prayer is especially relevant to our times!

So is the second petition, which is very practical. "Give us this day our daily bread" (vs. 11). Many have interpreted bread here in a "spiritualized" manner. It would appear that the consensus of modern scholarship, however, is toward a more mundane interpretation. This means He calls us to pray for the provision of our material needs. This is certainly the emphasis in the contemporary "materialist" readings of Scripture.

Today, where there are still millions — especially in Third World countries — who are hungry and exist on the brink of starvation, this petition is amazingly relevant!

When millions repeat this petition, they are literally praying for the provision of bread to fill their empty bellies and for other necessities of life — shelter, clothing, and education for their children. In the light of contemporary human need, it is sacrilege to spiritualize this important text!

The third petition has always presented difficulties for sensitive Christian souls. "And lead us not into temptation, but deliver us from evil" (vs. 13). Is this prayer really necessary? Many do not think that God would lead them into temptation. Once we realize that the word "tempt" can be used in a two-fold sense, we begin to appreciate its meaning. The word "tempt" can be mean to "entice to do evil" or "provoke to wrath," but it can also mean "to test or to try." Our faith grows stronger as it is tested in the crucible of life.

Essentially, then, we pray that we may not be led to the testing of our faith or our witness. Should it be necessary, however, we ask God to strengthen us to overcome the forces that threaten us. Continually, we note that there is a very strong element of confession. The word used here refers to deliberate sins that we have committed. In this prayer we seek pardon and forgiveness for our past sins.

This is followed by and linked to a word of intercession: "As we forgive our debtors" (vs. 12).

Our receiving of divine forgiveness is inextricably bound up with, if not dependent upon, our willingness to forgive others (Matthew 18:21-35). We who have, in Christ, experienced the joy of forgiveness of God should demonstrate a forgiving attitude to others. The Master urges us to think of the welfare of others in our prayer life.

This prayer is suitable for all situations. In the midst of the varied experiences of this transitory life, we can use it "in all the changing scenes of life, in troubles and in joy."

In situations where even the most experienced of spiritual giants have found it difficult to pray, they have turned to this model prayer and have discovered it to be an unfailing source of spiritual power.

Still, it is not enough for us simply to repeat *The Lord's Prayer* as often as possible. Rather, we should use it as a model or pattern for us in our prayer life. In our prayers we should include the elements of praise, thanksgiving, confession, petition, and intercession. By rounding out our focus, our prayer life will be greatly enriched and become a source of blessing both for ourselves and for those whom we bring before the throne of grace.

The Bible, then, is a very good, useful, and inexhaustible resource for prayer. Nearly every chapter provides the basis for prayer. We should, therefore, always have our Bible within reach when we pray, especially in our private devotions whether at home, at school, at the office, or at church.

Today, we are realizing more and more how important the Bible is as a major resource for prayer. The Rev. Dr. Donald E. Collins has written a book on the Bible as prayer, which is titled, *Like Trees That Grow Beside a Stream*.[2] The writer expresses the conviction that "the Bible is meant to be prayed as well as read, studied, and expounded upon . . ." His book is a very useful guide for improving your prayer life. I urge you to obtain a copy of Dr. Collins' book to inspire your devotional times.

Hymns Guide our Prayers

Christians from all walks of life, throughout the ages, have found another very useful resource in the development of their prayer life — the hymn book! This is not surprising. Many of our hymns are really prayers in song. As such, some hymns contain the various aspects of prayer that we have identified in our study of this vital subject.

Note for instance, that the opening verse of a well-known hymn is a prayer of praise:

> *Immortal, invisible, God only wise,*
> *In light inaccessible hid from our eyes,*
> *Most blessed, most glorious, the Ancient of Days,*
> *Almighty, victorious, Thy great name we praise.*[3]

A thoughtful prayer of thanksgiving is most intricately woven into the fabric of this beautiful harvest hymn:

> *We thank Thee, Lord, for sunshine, dew and rain*
> *Broadcast from heaven by Thine almighty hand*
> *Source of all life, unnumbered as the sand*
> *Bird, beast, and fish, herb, fruit, and golden grain.*
> *This unique fishermen's hymn begins with a prayer of petition:*
> *Hear us, O Lord, from heaven, Thy dwelling place:*
> *Like, them of old, in vain we toil all night,*
> *Unless with us Thou go, Who art the Light;*
> *Come, then, O Lord, that we may see Thy face.*[4]

Petition is also the burden of a well-known hymn, often used on patriotic occasions:

> *O God our help in ages past*
> *Our hope for years to come*
> *Be Thou our guard while troubles last*
> *And our eternal home.*[5]

Confession is at the heart of another well-known hymn, which, appropriately, is most often sung in evening services:

> *Dear Lord and Father of mankind,*
> *Forgive our foolish ways;*
> *Re-clothe us in our rightful mind;*
> *In purer lives Thy service find,*
> *In deeper reverence praise.*[6]

Here's another hymn which, from start to finish, is a prayer of intercession for the Church:

> *Jesus, with Thy Church abide;*
> *Be her Savior, Lord, and Guide,*
> *While on earth her faith is tried;*
> *We beseech Thee, hear us.*[7]

Finally, one of the most popular hymns of the Christian faith reminds us of the great spiritual resource that is available to us as we pray:

> *O what peace we often forfeit,*
> *O what needless pain we bear,*
> *All because we do not carry*
> *Everything to God in prayer!*[8]

Books on Prayer

Over the many centuries of the witness of the Church, many books of prayer have been published. The great giants of devotional life in all ages, as well as Christians representing all segments of society, have contributed to this vast spiritual treasure house. There are many such prayer books available to us, and others are being produced all the time. Some of these are listed at the end of this book. No doubt there are many others that you can use in developing your own prayer life.

Each of us is a unique being created by our God. We should use prayer books to stimulate us as we continue to strengthen our own devotional life and witness.

The cultivation of one's spiritual life is a very personal thing, especially when it comes to prayer!

Praying with Others

There is much to be gained spiritually by participating in prayer along with others. As has been repeated on several occasions, we are, by nature, gregarious. We love the company of fellow human beings. God Himself said, "It is not good that the man should be alone" (Genesis 2:18).

This is, indeed, very true of our prayer life. We are greatly strengthened in its development as we share with others the spiritual insights that have come to us in our own prayer experience. It is, therefore, most advantageous and advisable for us to pray often with others.

The old custom of having family prayer, which appeared to be in decline for some years, is now making a comeback. Many Christians proudly testify that they have regular family prayers. We should encourage this trend.

If you are a parent, you should have family prayers as often as possible. If you have small children, then remember to pray with them (and for them) every morning and at bedtime. Children are very receptive to prayer, and some have very inquiring minds. Indeed, sometimes they ask questions about prayer that we find hard to answer! Many leading Christians readily testify that they are strong in the faith today primarily because their parents began to teach them to pray while they were still little children.

The family that prays together stays together.

Attending Prayer Meetings

We have seen a revival of prayer meetings in our churches. In many churches, the week night prayer meeting is well attended and a source of spiritual power for the whole church.

I suggest that Christians attend prayer meeting at least one night per week. Attending a Sunday morning worship service is not enough. We should set apart at least one night per week when we offer prayer as part of a worshiping congregation.

One of the most significant features of contemporary Christianity is the growth of "the prayer cell movement" in the homes of members. Special prayer groups are springing up in many neighborhoods all over the world. Some of these are small and some are large. Some have prayers for an hour or two; others last through the night.

Indeed, we are hearing more and more about "all night prayer meetings" or "round the clock prayer meetings." Many devout Christians testify that their own prayer life has been greatly enriched by being in the company of fellow believers. The spiritual depth and the length of time devoted to prayer have both been enhanced by participation in prayer groups, sharing with others in an act of communion with God. Those who can barely pray for a few minutes on their own testify that as part of a prayer group, or "prayer band," they can continue for hours non-stop!

Yes, our prayer life is greatly enriched in the company of others. In prayer, as in so many other avenues of human endeavor, "iron sharpeneth iron" (Proverbs 27:17). If you would like to improve in this area, consider joining a prayer group that meets in your neighborhood.

Take the Initiative!

Suppose that there is not such a prayer group in your neighborhood. What should you do? Start one! You should seriously consider beginning a prayer group in your neighborhood or in the office where you work. Taking the initiative may be easier than you think. You may very well find that others, like yourself, are anxious to share in a prayer group of some kind.

Today people are faced with so many anxieties, problems, trials and tribulations, and so much loneliness that many are only too glad to participate in a prayer cell.

You can go about this in several ways. Perhaps the most effective way is for you to invite several neighbors to your home for prayer. Or you can address the need for prayer in light of community problems. You might begin by discussing with them some needs of the neighborhood, such as greater security, the need for a "clean up" project, etc.

As you discuss these needs, you may be led to join with your neighbors in prayer regarding these issues. Don't stop with prayer. You may be led to take action to improve the conditions of your community. Thus, your prayers may result in the transformation of your neighborhood, making it a better place for you and your neighbors. Indeed, praying together may lead to working for the improvement of the community. Prayer and work are inextricably bound up with each other!

It is essential that we work at our prayer life. Prayer is at once simple and most profound. Prayer can be learned, but *prayer is work!* Let us seek continually to improve our own prayer life. When we meet our neighbors, and friends and foes alike, let us invite them to share with us in prayer. Yes, let us challenge them with these words: *Come, let us pray!*

Endnotes

Chapter 1

1 Definitions of prayer given at a seminar on prayer held at St. Michael's Methodist Church, Boyd Sub-division, Nassau, Bahamas, sometime early in 1990.

2 Metropolitan Anthony, *Living Prayer* (Springfield, Illinois: Templegate, Publishers, 1966), p. 95. Metropolitan Anthony (known to many persons as Anthony Bloom) is a bishop of the Russian Orthodox Church in Great Britain. He is very well known for his preaching and works on the spiritual life and is often called upon to comment on religious and spiritual affairs. He appears regularly in religious broadcasts on radio and television.

3 Second verse of the hymn "Lord, Teach Us Now to Pray Aright" by James Montgomery 1771-1854.

Chapter 2

1 Popular gospel song written by singer and composer Andre Crouch.

2 St. Augustine of Hippo (354-430), recognized as one of the great Christian thinkers of all time, expressed the meaning of human existence in these immortal words, which are to be found at the beginning of his *Confessions*.

Chapter 3

1   Opening verse of a hymn of praise written by the German hymnologist Joachim Neander, 1650-1680, translated by Catherine Winkworth, 1829-1878, others.

Chapter 4

1   *Collins Dictionary*, L-Z, ed. D. Halsey (London: MacMillan, 1977), p. 753.

2   William Shakespeare.

3   Second Stanza of the hymn, "Come, My Soul, Thy Suit Prepare," by John Newton, 1725-1807.

4   Verse from the very well known hymn, "What a Friend We Have in Jesus," written by Joseph Medlicott Scriven, 1820-1886.

Chapter 5

1   The writer has dealt with the nature of David's sins elsewhere. See J. Emmette Weir.

2   See Dennis J. McCarthy, *Treaty and Covenant: Analecta Biblica* (Rome: Pontifical Biblical Institute, 1963).

3   Scholars have clearly demonstrated that the maintenance of justice in the sacral community was the major domestic responsibility of the king. The matter is dealt with carefully by John Gray in his illuminating book, *The Biblical Doctrine of the Reign of God* (Edinburgh: T. & T. Clark, 1979) and by Witlam in *The Just King* (Sheffield: JSOT, 1980). See also A.R. Johnson, *Sacral Kingship in Ancient Israel* (Cardiff: University Press, 1967).

4   See James Limburg, *The Prophets and the Powerless* (Atlanta: John Knox Press, 1977).

5   On this subject see the excellent, comprehensive study by N.H. Whybray (London: Student Christian Movement Press, 1967).

6   The significance of prayer as therapeutic process was discussed by Dr. Patrick Roberts in a very perceptive and illuminating address at a prayer seminar at Wesley Methodist Church, Nassau, Bahamas, in July 1991.

7   Those who would like to pursue exhaustive study of this psalm may consult the various commentaries, notably the major work by Author Weiser, *The Psalms.*

8   The writer was an Episcopal priest who had a deep social concern which was demonstrated throughout his ministry in a parish in New York.

Chapter 6

1   See Matthew 12:22; Mark 6:34-44; Luke 18:35-43; John 11.

2   On compassion see J. Emmette Weir, *The Challenge of Compassion* (Nassau Bahamas, 1978).

3   The late Paul Tillich, the famous German-American theologian, claimed that the major fear of contemporary man is the fear of meaninglessness.

4   William Shakespeare, *The Merchant of Venice.*

5   In many years of hospital visitation in a number of countries including the United States, the United Kingdom, Jamaica, and The Bahamas, the writer has very seldom come across anyone who refused a word of prayer. Indeed, in most cases, they welcomed a word of prayer and often requested it, especially when very ill!

6   With the rapid spread of AIDS, it is essential that Christians should include concerns for those suffering from this disease in their prayers of intercession. Pastors should be especially sensitive to the needs of persons suffering from AIDS and include special prayers for them in preparing orders of service.

Chapter 7

1 This account of the healing of her son is recorded by his mother Kweda Sinclair in "The Methodist Messenger" Nassau, Bahamas 1989, p. 10. This dramatic, inspiring story demonstrates that the healing power of God is still available to us today and should prove a source of comfort and encouragement to many who are suffering now.

2 On the life of Thomas Coke, see John Poxon, *Thomas Coke* (Kingston, Jamaica, 1989).

3 This well-known meditation, "The Prayer of Serenity," has been a source of inspiration to many throughout the ages.

4 Sermon preached by the late Rev. A. E. Brown at a Baptist church in the Parish of Portland, Jamaica sometime in 1956.

5 Sermon preached by the Rev. Dr. Colin Archer at Ebenezer Methodist Church, Nassau, Bahamas on Sunday July 28, 1991.

Chapter 8

1 The late Isaac Bashevis Singer was a distinguished American Jewish writer and poet. He had already made a considerable contribution in literary pursuits in his native Poland, when he migrated to the United States. There he gradually earned recognition as an interesting and provocative writer, publishing works in both Yiddish and English.

2. Donald Collins, *The Trees That Grow Beside a Stream* (Nashville: Abingdon Press, 1991).

3 Opening Stanza of the well known hymn by William Chalmers Smith 1824-1908.

4 These verses are extracted from a harvest hymn which comes to us from the Isle of Man, located off the coast of England, Great Britain. Written by William Henry Gill (1839-1923), it vividly describes the simple, rustic lifestyle of a hard-working people who eked out a living by means of peasant farming

and fishing. This hymn, marked by a deep abiding faith in the Providence of God, "The Bountiful Provider," has proved to be popular at harvest services in churches in the Caribbean, where socio-economic conditions of many rural communities are very similar to those reflected in the hymn.

5 Opening stanza of the well known hymn by the famous hymn writer, Isaac Watts, 1674-1748.

6 Opening stanza of hymn by the well known American poet, John Greenleaf Whittier, 1807-1892.

7 Opening stanza of hymn written by Theomad Benson Pollock, 1836- 1896.

8 Extract from the opening verse of the favorite hymn that has proved a great source of consolation in times of bereavement, "What a Friend We Have in Jesus."

9 See Appendix.

10 There can be no doubt that prayer, like so many other spheres of endeavor, is greatly enriched by sharing with others. Indeed, while some are able to spend many hours in prayer in solitude, which is often necessary in the cultivation of the spiritual life, most confess that by joining in corporate prayer their own spiritual development is greatly facilitated. This is not surprising, considering the essentially gregarious nature of man. As one Christian leader John Donne puts it, "No man is an island." Or, in the profound words of Scripture, "It is not good that the man should be alone" (Genesis 2:18).

Appendix

Growing in prayer is a life-long experience! We should be constantly seeking to grow in this aspect of our spiritual development. This book, originally prepared for the observance of the Bahamas National Year Of Call To Prayer (marking 500 years of Christian witness in the western hemisphere), is just a beginning!

The reader is encouraged to continue to develop his or her prayer life by making use of the many resources that are available. Throughout the ages many have felt the call of God to devote their gifts, time, and energies to the development of their prayer life, and they have contributed to the spiritual treasure of the church. Some of these resources are listed below. Do make use of some, if not all, of them!

Major Works on Prayer

The various denominations all have their own prayer books and devotional resources, and the reader may consult his or her spiritual leader for the relevant works. Many books and other resources on prayer (such as audio and video tapes, films, cards, etc.) are produced by the churches. Organizations such as The Upper Room of Nashville, Tennessee; The International Bible Reading Association, Robert Denholm House, Surrey, England; The International Bible Societies; and the Scripture Union of Great Britain publish very good material on prayer.

Books on Prayer

A Chain of Prayer Throughout the Ages. This classic work has inspired and strengthened many people from all walks of life.

Metropolitan, Anthony (Anthony Bloom). *Living Prayer.* Springfield, Illinois: Templegate Publishers.

Albans, Helen. *Praying with Sticky Fingers.* London: Methodist Publishing House. Lesson on how to pray with small children.

Allen, Charles. *God's Psychiatry.* Nashville: Broadman Press.

Baillie, John. *A Diary of Private Prayer.* Edinburgh: St. Andrew Press.

Barclay, William. *Prayers for the Plain Man.* London: SCM Press.

Barclay, William. *Prayers for Health and Healing.* London: SCM Press.

Boyd, Malcolm. *Are You Running with Me, Jesus?* New York: Holt, Rinehart & Winston.

Champlin, Joseph. *Behind Closed Doors: A Handbook on How to Pray.* New York: Paulist Press.

Collins, Donald. *The Trees That Grow Beside a Stream.* Nashville: Abingdon Press.

Community of Taize. *Praying Together in Word and Song.* Oxford: A.R. Mowbray.

Copeland, Kenneth. *Prayer: Your Foundation for Success.* Fort Worth, TX: KCP Publications.

Coupland, Susan. *Beginning to Pray in Old Age.* Cambridge, MA.: Cowley Press.

Davidson, Graema J. *Anyone Can Pray: A Guide to Methods of Christian Prayer.* New York: Paulist Press.

Davis, Elisabeth. *For Each Day a Prayer.* New York: Dodge Publishing Co.

Eadie, Donald. *Praying Now.* Peterborough: Methodist Publishing House.

Ellis, Neil. *The Power of the Blood.* Nassau, Bahamas.

Green, Thomas H. *When the Well Runs Dry.* Notre Dame, Indiana: Ave Maria Press.

Gribble, Robert F. *Our Stewardship of Prayer.* Published by the Stewardship Department, Presbyterian Church of the U.S.

George, A. Raymond. *Communion with God in the New Testament.* Peterborough: Methodist Publishing House.

Hassell, David J. *Healing the Ache of Alienation: Praying Through and Beyond Bitterness*. New York: The Paulist Press.

Higgins, John J. *Merton's Theology of Prayer*. Spencer, MA.: Cistercian Publications.

Irwin, Kevin. *Liturgy, Prayer & Spirituality*. New York: Paulist Press.

Jenkins, Daniel Thomas. *Prayer and the Service of God*. New York: Morehouse Gorham Co.

Kallinger, John. *Bread for the Wilderness, Wine for the Journey: The Miracle of Prayer and Meditation*. Waco, TX: Word Books.

Merton, Thomas. *Contemplative Prayer*. New York: Herder & Herder.

Mensies, L. (Editor). *Life as Prayer and Other Writings of Evelyn Underhill*. Harrisburg, PA: Morehouse Publishing Co.

Murray, Andrew. *With Christ in the School of Prayer*. Springdale, PA: Whitaker House.

Pickard, Jan S. & Edwards, Maureen. *Oceans of Prayer: An Anthology of Prayers & Meditations from the World Church*. Peterborough: Methodist Publishing House.

Peterson, Eugene H. *Answering God: The Psalms as Tools for Prayer*. San Francisco: Harper & Row.

Price, Fredrick. *How to Obtain Strong Faith*. Tulsa, OK: Harrison House.

Quoist, Michael. *Prayers for Christian Living*. London: SCM Press.

Contemporary Prayers, Relevant and Down to Earth. Especially appropriate for youth services, meetings, devotions at camps, etc.

Torry, R.A. *How to Obtain Fullness of Power*. Springdale, PA: Whitaker House.

Sangster, William. *Lord, Teach Us to Pray*. Springdale, PA: Whitaker House. See Chapter Four on "The Power of Prayer."

Whitney, Doris E. *To Be Honest, Lord*. Peterborough: Methodist Publishing House.

Wright, John H. *A Theology of Prayer*. Pueblo Press.

About the Author

Dr. Joseph Emmette Augustus Weir, a native of the Bahamas Islands, studied at the United Theological College of the West Indies, Kingston, Jamaica. He has earned a Bachelor of Divinity from London University, Master of Sacred Theology from Christian Theological Seminary, and Doctor of Philosophy from the University of Aberdeen. He is presently a member of the faculty of Templeton Theological Seminary. A Methodist minister, he has served in pastorates in Jamaica, Eleuthera, and New Providence.

Send all prayer requests and inquiries to:

Dr. Emmette Weir
P. O. Box N-3732
Nassau, Bahamas

Additional copies of *Come, Let Us Pray!* are available from your local bookstore or from Pneuma Life Publishing.

OTHER BOOKS FROM
Pneuma Life Publishing

Why? Because You Are Anointed
by T.D. Jakes

Why do the righteous, who have committed their entire lives to obeying God, seem to endure so much pain and experience such conflict? These perplexing questions have plagued and bewildered Christians for ages. In this anointed and inspirational new book, Bishop T.D. Jakes provocatively and skillfully answers these questions and many more as well as answering the "why" of the anointed. *Workbook also available*

Water in the Wilderness
by T.D. Jakes

Just before you apprehend your greatest conquest, expect the greatest struggle. Many are perplexed who encounter this season of adversity. This book will show you how to survive the worst of times with the greatest of ease, and will cause fountains of living water to spring out of the parched, sun–drenched areas in your life. This word is a refreshing stream in the desert for the weary traveler.

The Harvest
by T.D. Jakes

God's heart beats for lost and dying humanity. The Church, however, has a tremendous shortage of sold-out, unselfish Christians committed to the salvation and discipleship of the lost. This disillusioned generation hungers for lasting reality. Are we ready to offer them eternal hope in Jesus Christ? Without a passion for holiness, sanctification, and evangelism, we will miss the greatest harvest of the ages. God has ordained the salvation of one final crop of souls and given us the privilege of putting in the sickle. Allow God to set you ablaze. Seize the opportunity of a lifetime and become an end-time laborer in the Church's finest hour! *Workbook also available*

Help Me! I've Fallen
by T.D. Jakes

"Help! I've fallen, and I can't get up." This cry, made popular by a familiar television commercial, points out the problem faced by many Christians today. Have you ever stumbled and fallen with no hope of getting up? Have you been wounded and hurt by others? Are you so far down you think you'll never stand again? Don't despair. All Christians fall from time to time. Life knocks us off balance, making it hard – if not impossible – to get back on our feet. The cause of the fall is not as important as what we do while we're down. T.D. Jakes explains how and Whom to ask for help. In a struggle to regain your balance, this book is going to be your manual to recovery! Don't panic. This is just a test!

Becoming A Leader
by Myles Munroe

Many consider leadership to be no more than staying ahead of the pack, but that is a far cry from what leadership is. Leadership is deploying others to become as good as or better than you are. Within each of us lies the potential to be an effective leader. *Becoming A Leader* uncovers the secrets of dynamic leadership that will show you how to be a leader in your family, school, community, church and job. No matter where you are or what you do in life this book can help you to inevitably become a leader. Remember: it is never too late to become a leader. As in every tree there is a forest, so in every follower there is a leader. ***Workbook also available***

This is My Story
by Candi Staton

This is My Story is a touching autobiography about a gifted young child who rose from obscurity and poverty to stardom and wealth. With a music career that included selling millions of albums and topping the charts came a life of brokenness, loneliness, and despair. This book will make you cry and laugh as you witness one woman's search for success and love. Candi Staton is also the author of *"I Didn't Raise Him to be a Criminal."*

The God Factor
by James Giles

Is something missing in your life? Do you find yourself at the mercy of your circumstances? Is your self-esteem at an all-time low? Are your dreams only a faded memory? You could be missing the one element that could make the difference between success and failure, poverty and prosperity, and creativity and apathy. Knowing God supplies the creative genius you need to reach your potential and realize your dream. You'll be challenged as James Giles shows you how to tap into your God-given genius, take steps toward reaching your goal, pray big and get answers, eat right and stay healthy, prosper economically and personally, and leave a lasting legacy for your children.

Making the Most of Your Teenage Years
by David Burrows

Most teenagers live for today. Living only for today, however, can kill you. When teenagers have no plan for their future, they follow a plan that someone else devised. Unfortunately, this plan often leads them to drugs, sex, crime, jail, and an early death. How can you make the most of your teenage years? Discover who you really are – and how to plan for the three phases of your life. You can develop your skill, achieve your dreams, and still have fun.

The African Cultural Heritage Topical Bible

The African Cultural Heritage Topical Bible is a quick and convenient reference Bible. It has been designed for use in personal devotions as well as group Bible studies. It's the newest and most complete reference Bible designed to reveal the Black presence in the Bible and highlight the contributions and exploits of Blacks from the past to present. It's a great tool for students, clergy, teachers — practically anyone seeking to learn more about the Black presence in Scripture, but didn't know where to start.

The African Cultural Heritage Topical Bible contains:
• Over 395 easy to find **topics**
• **3,840 verses** that are systematically organized
• A comprehensive listing of Black Inventions
• Over **150 pages** of Christian Afrocentric articles on Blacks in the Bible, Contributions of Africa, African Foundations of Christianity, Culture, Identity, Leadership, and Racial Reconciliation written by Myles Munroe, Wayne Perryman, Dr. Leonard Lovett, Dr. Trevor L. Grizzle, James Giles, and Mensa Otabil.

Available in KJV and NIV versions

Daily Moments With God In Quietness and Confidence
by Jacqueline E. McCullough

As you journey into God's presence, take this volume with you. Evangelist Jacqueline E. McCullough has compiled her very own treasury of poetry, punctuated phrases, and sermonettes to inspire you to trust, love, and obey the Lord Jesus Christ. Are you hurtling through life at a hectic pace, overwhelmed by problems and lacking peace? Has your busy schedule cut short your devotions? Has this noisy world dulled your ability to hear God's voice? *Daily Moments With God* will direct your thoughts toward God, shed insight on the Scriptures, and encourage you to meditate on life-changing truths. As your spirit soars in prayer, praise, and worship, the presence and power of God will transform you.

Single Life
by Earl D. Johnson

A book that candidly addresses the spiritual and physical dimensions of the single life is finally here. *Single Life* shows the reader how to make their singleness a celebration rather than a burden. This positive approach to singles uses enlightening examples from Apostle Paul, himself a single, to beautifully portray the dynamic aspects of the single life. The book gives fresh insight on practical issues such as coping with sexual desires, loneliness, and preparation for your future mate. Written in a lively style, the author admonishes singles to seek first the kingdom of God and rest assured in God's promise to supply their needs... including a life partner!

Flaming Sword
by Tai Ikomi
Scripture memorization and meditation bring tremendous spiritual power, however many Christians find it to be an uphill task. Committing Scriptures to memory will transform the mediocre Christian to a spiritual giant. This book will help you to become addicted to the powerful practice of Scripture memorization and help you obtain the victory that you desire in every area of your life. *Flaming Sword* is your pathway to spiritual growth and a more intimate relationship with God.

The Call of God
by Jefferson Edwards
The Call of God will help you to; have clarity from God as to what ministry involves; be able to identify and affirm the call in your life; determine which stage you are in your call from God; remove confusion in relation to the processing of a call or the making of the person; understand the development of the anointing to fulfill your call.

The Minister's Topical Bible
by Derwin Stewart
The Minister's Topical Bible covers every aspect of the ministry providing quick and easy access to Scriptures in a variety of ministry related topics. This handy reference tool can be effectively used in leadership training, counseling, teaching, sermon preparation, and personal study.

The Believer's Topical Bible
by Derwin Stewart
The Believer's Topical Bible covers every aspect of a Christian's relationship with God and man, providing biblical answers and solutions for many challenges. It is a quick, convenient, and thorough reference Bible that has been designed for use in personal devotions and group Bible studies. With over 3,800 verses systematically organized under 240 topics, it is the largest devotional-topical Bible available in the New International Version and the King James Version.

*Available at your local bookstore
or by contacting:*

Pneuma Life Publishing

P.O. Box 10612

Bakersfield, CA 93389-0612